SCOOTINAMERICA-INS.

MW00886392

Copyright © 2016 by Adam Sandoval

CHAPTER ONE

"The short successes that can be gained in a brief time and without difficulty are not worth much."—Henry Ford 1922

It was close to two a.m. as I rode my old dusty black 1996 Harley-Davidson through the California hills just above Malibu with my little dog Scooter tucked warmly into the front of my jacket. It was cold and wet and every one of my muscles had begun to give way to the weight of gravity. We'd been going non-stop for over eighteen hours and I had just finally had enough. I was done. I'd given up on the idea of a warm bed and solid night of dreams by that point, but I had to find a place to at least try and close my eyes. We came to a curve in the main road and off to my right I saw a narrow gravel path that stretched back into the hills. I turned onto it and rode deeper into the darkness until I spotted a berm. I stopped there and we got off the bike. The wind was gusting and a continuous cold mist rained down on top of me. I couldn't tell from where I stood if we were visible from the main road so I had to walk back down and take a look. By the time I found an acceptable spot that would shield us from unwanted guests, I'd walked up to that miserable road and back four times. Each time I came back and moved the bike just a little further back until at last I couldn't see it from the road at all.

When I got back the last time I unrolled the tarp and tied one end of it to the bike. I spent some time looking for some soft ground to stake it to but there was nothing around. Ultimately I stretched it out as taut as I could and rested it against the rain soaked ground, stacking the gear that I carry on the bike on top of it. We climbed in at last in the hopes of resting our weary heads.

I drifted off quickly even as the wind beat out a rhythm on the tarp. For the next hour or so it would occasionally beat hard enough that the tarp would ripple and tug until it pulled loose of

SCOOTINAMERICA-INSIDE MY HELMET

the gear I had stacked on it. Several times I woke up to it slapping me in the face and I had to go back out in the cold and readjust everything. Each time I got back into the lean-to it would only take seconds for me to drift back off into sleep. I don't know how much time passed before Scooter began to howl. Scooter's bark is normally high-pitched like all small dogs…But that night there was something else in it…it was screeching and squealing and by the way he was shaking and pawing at me, I knew whatever he sensed, heard or smelled was going to be trouble.

Once again I stepped out of the tarp. The darkness of the hills around me was the kind that robbed you of your vision and heightened your other senses. The sound of the wind as it hit the tarp was like the rhythmic pounding of a drum and once we were outside even though he was tucked into the safety of my jacket, Scooter's screams became even more intense. I tried to calm him as I listened in the darkness to what sounded like the echoes of yips and barks off in the distance. I decided it was a pack of coyotes but because of the weather and the surrounding mountains and canyons, it echoed and I couldn't tell how close they were. We went back inside my little makeshift tent and I continued to try and calm Scooter down. I was afraid the noise he was making was like a dinner bell to the hungry predators outside.

Scooter couldn't seem to calm down and only minutes after going back inside I heard a new rustling sound to add to the other noises of the night. At first I thought it was just more wind…but Scooter was really losing it and the next howl from the coyotes came from what sounded like only feet away. I was afraid they were coming for Scooter. I was sure that I was too big to be on their menu, but my little buddy was just about the right size. I had to go out and see if I could scare them off. This time I took a flashlight with me and when I shined it around it eventually landed on two shiny yellow orbs hanging in the air about six feet away. My stomach clenched as another pair appeared and then another. Four…maybe five coyotes stood perfectly still, their glowing eyes watching me and the wiggling and noise that was still coming from inside my jacket with voracious interest. A chill ran through me and the only thing I could think of at that moment was that I had to

SCOOTINAMERICA-INSIDE MY HELMET

protect Scooter. I started yelling and they startled and moved back. I kept yelling…I was telling them to go away, get back, leave us alone…anything that came to mind and some of it just came out of my mouth without passing through my mind at all. Finally they turned tail and ran. I wasn't sure how far they went, but I wasn't going after them. I did however realize that this was one of those "moments." It was one of the reasons that I'd ached to make this trip. It was one of those experiences that would etch itself into my memory forever…but I'd never be able to describe it. With one hand on Scooter I dug out my Go-Pro and with the other frozen hand I scrambled to hook it up along the side of my bike. I pointed it in the direction of the canyon. I waited a few beats and then Scooter and I climbed back into the lean-to. I listened in the darkness and tried to dissimilate the difference between the sounds of the relentless wind and those of the hungry predators that I didn't doubt would be back.

For probably what was only a few seconds it felt like time was standing still. Sleep was relentless though and it wasn't long before it claimed me again. I don't know how much time passed this time but it didn't feel like much. Scooter warned me first with his squalls and almost immediately I began to hear the yips and howls of the coyotes…they were close, again. With fear in my heart for Scooter, I made sure he was tucked tightly against me and out of sight and I went back outside with the flashlight. They were back and this time even closer. Once again I began to yell and holler. I can't even remember now what I said, but I'm pretty sure it included just about every obscenity I've ever learned. I sounded like a maniac, but that was the idea…maybe if they thought I was crazy, they would go away. They bared their teeth and I could hear the growls grow deeper in their throats competing with the noise that Scooter was making. I had to advance towards them as I yelled; knowing the very thing they wanted was attached to me. I couldn't let Scooter slip out from my jacket. That would be like offering him up on a platter. It took some time but once again I chased them off far enough that their howls echoed off the walls of the canyon below us. This time before I went back underneath the tarp, I picked up a big stick that happened to be lying in our campsite and took it inside with us.

SCOOTINAMERICA-INSIDE MY HELMET

I was asleep once again when they came back. Scooter's bark had become almost hoarse with panic at this point. I picked up the big stick and stepped out of the tarp with Scooter still protectively cradled against my chest. There were five of them. Two of them had circled around in front of the lean-to and the other three were around on the other side. It looked like they had an ambush planned. I tried yelling again, but this time it didn't seem to be working. I could feel Scooter's little heart thudding against me and mine was pounding out a rhythm right alongside it. I raised the stick and took a step towards the two in front. As I did they stepped back but the three on the side advanced. I turned sideways and with my yells I incorporated a swing of my make-shift weapon. I didn't want to hit them; I was just hoping to once again scare them away. We did a little dance for a while. I'd yell and swing and they'd skitter around, barking and growling. Their yellow eyes stayed on me, not wavering, and I did my best to keep my eyes on all of them.

The moment of truth finally came and they moved in closer. They were an arm's length away and it was a do or die moment. Not that I thought I was going to die…but if I gave up I knew Scooter would, and that was not an option. I pulled back the stick and yelled one last time. They advanced again and this time I swung. I connected with the side of the coyote's head that was closest to me. He screamed and whimpered and the sound of his pain seemed to motivate the others to scatter and run off into the night. I stood there in a semi-state of shock for several minutes afterwards and that was the moment that I had to ask myself…*What the fuck am I doing here?*

This was our campsite that night

CHAPTER TWO

"Life always offers you a second chance, it's called tomorrow."--Unknown

Thinking back, I would have to say that I could trace the beginnings of my misery on the mountain that night back to a warm bed in Florida with a beautiful woman. Most people think of intimacy as sex, but that's truly only one way a couple can be intimate. Being with someone that you can be completely free with to talk about your dreams and your hopes and even your insecurities…that's intimacy as well. My wife Laura and I spent a lot of intimate moments wrapped up in each other's arms talking about everything from mundane chores that needed to be done to our dreams for the future. One dream in particular often came up as we talked…the idea of traveling around the United States on our motorcycles. It was one of those dreams that started with the foundation of something I'd always had in the back of my mind and was built upon with each pillow talk we had over the course of many months. I can't recall the specifics of every one of our conversations but it started something like this:

"I want to travel; I want us to take a road trip on the bikes…a really long trip, maybe across the United States?" I told her.

She propped herself up on her elbow and looked at my face. "Seriously?"

"Yeah, why not?"

"That sounds like fun. What about work?"

"I haven't thought it completely through yet, but I'm sure we could afford it if we did it cheaply…you know, without four star hotels and fancy meals."

SCOOTINAMERICA-INSIDE MY HELMET

She laughed. "Okay, three star hotels will work. Scooter sure would like it" Scooter was our little Chihuahua. We'd rescued him from a puppy mill when he was only about eight weeks old.

"Imagine it, the open road just you and me and Scooter." Scooter loved to ride on the bike with me. I could see him loving the trip as much as we did.

"That sounds amazing."

"Doesn't it? We would definitely have to sit down and hash out the details, but I seriously think we could do this."

Meanwhile, our daily lives went on. The bar we had bought wasn't doing well financially and I'd recently taken a job with Fighter's Source as COO and I had to do quite a bit of traveling. Laura didn't like me traveling so much and I was tired of it myself. We'd moved to Florida after I'd gotten out of the MMA fight promoting business and we had sunk a lot of money into our home and the bar. When Fighter's Source first offered me the position, I'd turned it down…but the deal kept getting sweeter so eventually I accepted it with the idea that it wouldn't be forever. One lazy afternoon while Laura and I lay in bed I said,

"What if we did the ride for charity?"

"What charity would we chose?"

"I haven't done any research yet, but I know there are a lot of military charities out there." One of my biggest regrets at that point in my life was that I'd never joined the military. It had always been a thought in the back of my mind. I'd even seriously considered it after Laura and I got together. By that time I was already well into my thirties though and that, coupled with the fact that Laura really didn't like it when I traveled a lot kept me from doing it then. When I started thinking seriously about doing this trip, I wondered if I could find a way to serve after all.

"What do you think?"

SCOOTINAMERICA-INSIDE MY HELMET

"Yeah, it sounds nice, Adam."

"I've also been giving some thought to how we might market it." I'd actually given it a lot of thought. Marketing was one of my specialties and I had about a hundred ideas.

"For sponsors and donations?" she asked.

"Yeah. I thought our catch phrase could be something like, "The couple that rides together, stays together."

"Cute."

Maybe not that day but in conversations to come, I talked about social media marketing and logo's and even maybe doing photo shoots leading up to the ride. Laura is beautiful. She's one of those women who literally knock the oxygen out of your lungs the first time you see her. She has the kind of face and body that could have easily graced any magazine cover in the country. I could already picture the promotions.

The more I talked about this and thought about it and actually started doing some research into it the more excited I became. I could already picture it in my head and at first I thought that Laura could too. When the realization crept in that I'd been the one doing most if not all of the talking I began to wonder if she'd lost her enthusiasm for it and she just didn't want to hurt my feelings. It wasn't that she was saying anything negative, or discouraging, it was that she just wasn't really saying anything at all. But I wasn't willing to lose hope…yet.

My wife had an enormous sense of adventure and it was one of the things I found so attractive about her. My own sense of adventure and the spontaneous lifestyle I was leading when she met me was attractive to her as well. I'd made a lot of money with MMA (mixed Martial Arts) in its infancy and with my entrepreneurial activities on the side. When I met Laura I was working hard and playing harder. We were together for six years before we got married and for most of those six years we played

SCOOTINAMERICA-INSIDE MY HELMET

hard together and lived lavishly. The move to Florida had been about settling down and having more time for each other. The money wasn't there for the extravagances we'd had before, but we were definitely not poor. We were still pursuing another dream of ours as well at the time, shopping for a farmhouse outside of town. That was another dream, to get out of the city and into the country, away from all the people where we could raise animals.

It didn't dawn on me until other problems in our relationship began to pop up that maybe it wasn't that particular dream she'd lost interest in…maybe it was that she'd begun to lose faith in me, faith in my ability to execute on my dreams as I had in the past. Things seemed to grow cooler between us all the time and no matter how hard I tried to put the intimacy back into our relationship…it seemed that we grew further apart. I was hopeful and encouraged when we got a call telling us our offer was accepted on one of the properties we really loved.

It came right around the time I was scheduled to fly out to Syracuse for work. The night before, Laura and I went out to the property with a bottle of champagne and we spent the night under the stars, toasting to our future. The next morning Laura dropped me off at the airport gave me a passionate kiss and I left for New York happy and feeling like things were going to be okay between us. I knew that I was willing to do whatever it took. I wasn't ready to give up on us or our dreams. I still felt like I had the ability to execute.

****

The event I was working in New York was a broadcasted MMA event. During the day I was going to be constantly busy with setting up and making sure that everything was in place. Laura knew that and that's what surprised me the most when I got a text from her out of the blue that said,

SCOOTINAMERICA-INSIDE MY HELMET

"Do you think we're going to make it?" At first I just thought it was strange timing for such a deep question. I text back,

"Of course I do. Why are you asking me that?"

A second later I got, "I just don't want to lose you." Lose me? What is she talking about?

"I'm not going anywhere. I love you."

"I love you too."

Off and on throughout the morning I got random messages like that and then that afternoon she called me. I had to excuse myself from work and take it because these text messages were driving me crazy. I hoped that she was going to tell me what was wrong. At the very least I hoped I could reassure her that things were okay on my end.

"Hey baby, what's going on?"

"I don't know. I'm just afraid of losing you, Adam."

"Laura, where is this coming from? I don't understand. I have no intention of leaving you."

"Things are just different between us."

"I know, but they're going to get better. I'm not willing to give up, okay? I love you."

"I love you too."

She seemed okay when we hung up and I went back to work but it wasn't long before she started texting me again, saying similar, if not the same things. It was starting to really get to me. I had no idea what was going on with her. I was having a hard time keeping my mind on work and my CFO noticed and asked me about it.

SCOOTINAMERICA-INSIDE MY HELMET

"Is everything okay?"

I thought about just telling him it was and letting it go at that but before I realized it, I was saying, "I'm not sure…my wife is acting a little strange."

"Strange, like she's sick or something?"

"No, she's just saying some strange things about losing me…I have no idea what's going on but it's making my head go places that I don't want to go."

"Like?"

"I'm starting to wonder if she's cheating on me." I felt anxious just saying that out loud. Did I really think she was cheating? No…but something was going on.

He did his best to encourage me that things were probably not as bad as they seemed on the phone. I agreed with him and told myself that worrying about things I didn't know to be true was a waste of energy. But none of that stopped the anxiety from coiling in my belly like a snake as I finished out the day.

SCOOTINAMERICA-INSIDE MY HELMET

**Me presenting Josh Kasee with $10,000-win
bonus after his fight**

CHAPTER THREE

"All great changes are preceded by chaos"—Deepak Chopra

That night when I called Laura she sounded like she was feeling better. I was relieved by that, but still couldn't help but wonder what had brought all of that on in the first place.

"So, can we talk about the text messages and phone call?" I asked her.

"No. I don't want to talk about it tonight. I don't want to talk about it on the phone." I wanted to argue with her. Being that far from her and knowing something was not right was killing me. I didn't think that trying to force her to talk to me was going to do anything but upset us both again, so I let it go…for now.

I didn't sleep well again that night for worrying, and the next day things snowballed from weird into really bizarre. It was the day of the event and in the middle of being surrounded by cranes, lighting, sound, and film equipment that she called me and completely fell apart on the phone. She was telling me again that she thought she was going to lose me and this time she was crying. I stopped what I was doing and went outside. I sat down outside and talked to her for over an hour. I hated hearing how upset she was. I wished that I was home so I could hold her and convince her that everything was going to be okay. I told her for at least the tenth time in three days,

"I have no intentions of leaving you. I would be willing to fight for us if I had to, you know that. I love you so much. Will you please tell me what this is about?"

"I don't know. I just feel like we're not going to be okay."

"Every time you have that feeling remind yourself that I love you, okay? Do you love me?"

SCOOTINAMERICA-INSIDE MY HELMET

"Yes, I love you. I love you more than anything in this world"

"That's all we need. We'll be okay. Please try to stop worrying."

"I'll try. I hate it when you're not here Adam. I just can't stand being alone."

"I know. One more day and I'll be back. As soon as I am, we'll sit down and talk, okay?"

By the time we hung up she was a lot calmer, but I still couldn't help but wonder, "*What the hell is going on?*"

When I finished working the show that night, I called her back. She didn't pick up so I left her a message telling her again that I loved her and that we'd talk when I got home. I had a hard time sleeping that night, worrying about her. I would have felt better if I could have heard her voice before I went to bed. I knew she had to work early though so I just assumed that she was sleeping.

The next morning I was on my way to go break down equipment when she called me back.

"I had to leave work because I had an anxiety attack," she said bluntly.

"What? Why?"

"I don't know," her voice sounded shaky as she went on to say, "I felt so bad, I couldn't breathe." I heard her voice crack and I really didn't want to upset her so I said,

"Okay, it's okay…I'll be home tonight. We'll talk tonight, okay? Everything's going to be alright."

SCOOTINAMERICA-INSIDE MY HELMET

"Move away with me, Adam." Her voice was suddenly pleading.

"Move away where?" This was getting stranger all the time.

"Alaska. Let's go to Alaska and just start all over."

"Alaska? Really?"

"Please, move away with me." I didn't have any desire to go to Alaska, but I said,

"Sure, okay. If that's what you want I'll move with you to Alaska. I'll move with you anywhere. I love you." I wasn't just blowing smoke. I would do whatever it took to make her happy, even if that was Alaska. That at least seemed to calm her down…for a while. Once everything was broken down and cleaned up I had to ride in a big van with the rest of the crew from Syracuse to Manhattan. While I was in the van for a three hour ride I started getting rude, mean text messages from her. My head was spinning…I don't ever remember being so confused. I was also filled with anxiety because there was no way that I was going to call her back and have this conversation with all of these people around me. I text her and said,

"We'll talk about this when I get home."

Her text back said, "I have to work in the morning. I don't want to talk about it when you get home."

At that point she had me feeling like I was losing my mind a little bit. It was obvious something big was going on…but what, was still the question. I wanted to argue with her and tell her that we needed to talk. I wanted to at least call and talk to her about it, but I couldn't do either. She'd already left work because of the anxiety attack. I didn't want her to go in the next morning sleep-deprived. My last text to her that night said,

SCOOTINAMERICA-INSIDE MY HELMET

"Just go to bed and rest tonight, baby. We'll talk tomorrow. I'll get a ride home from the airport don't worry about picking me up, okay?"

I didn't hear back from her again and the silence drove me nearly as crazy as everything else. It was late when I got into Florida. I hoped that she just went to bed and in the morning she'd be feeling better. I didn't call her because I didn't want to wake her up. I called a friend of mine who had a car service to give me a ride home and on the way home I stopped so I could buy Laura some flowers. With flowers in hand I arrived home around eleven-thirty that night to Scooter who was home alone. This was the point where I did everything in my power to convince myself to not let my mind jump to the worst case scenario. She told me during one of our phone conversations that she was going out with some friends while I was out of town. I'd asked her who she was going out with and she'd told me, Cathy and Charlene. They're both really good friends of ours and so I was hoping that would be where I could find her.

I scooped up Scooter and he and I got on my bike and I headed towards Cathy's house to see if she was there. As I drove through town I passed the grocery store. It was closed and the parking lot was virtually empty. There was one car in the lot and it looked an awful lot like mine. I drove up next to it and parked. I got off the bike and looked around. It was undeniably my car. Keeping the bad thoughts at bay had just gotten a whole lot harder.

My thoughts began to race as I tried to decide what to do. Should I wait for her to come back so that I could see first-hand what she'd been up to? If I waited to confront her at home, would she lie to me? Even if she told me the truth, would I believe her at this point? With my stomach in knots I got back on my bike and raced Scooter home. I was panicking that I wouldn't get back in time, but I had no idea what time she would show up…or with whom and I wanted Scooter to be at home, safe and sound. After dropping him off, I raced back downtown and I was both relieved and sickened by the fact that the car was still there. The emotions in my body were at war with each other. By this time it was after

17

SCOOTINAMERICA-INSIDE MY HELMET

midnight and I'd definitively decided to wait and see if, when and how she got back to the car.

I was tired from four long days of being away from home…but at the same time I was filled with adrenaline. I wanted to be wrong about the ideas that were floating around in my head. I wanted her to be at a friend's house which was what I was sure she'd tell me later if I went home and waited for her there. For the next four hours my emotions ran rampant as I did push-ups on the sidewalk and used a potato of all things that I found in the alley as a stress ball. I tossed it up and down as I paced and tried to calm myself down with a constant dialogue going through my head,

"I'm not going to flip-out. I'm going to beat his ass. I'm not going to beat anyone's ass, I'm going to make sure she sees me and then wait at home for the confrontation. I'm not going to let her see me and then wait at home and see what she tells me. I don't know for sure that she's cheating. She'll lie about it and that will just make things worse. It's three fucking a.m. what else would she be doing?"

It was just about four a.m. when a pick-up truck drove into the parking lot next to her car. She cracked the door open and the light came on. The truck was facing me and I could clearly see a man in the driver's seat. My pulse was racing and my body was already preparing for a fight. I still hadn't made the decision to go or stay when it was suddenly taken out of my hands. She leaned over and I watched as she kissed this guy…it felt like a fist was crushing my intestines. I lost any self-control I had maintained up to that point and I ran across the street. Before I got there Laura stepped out of the truck. She was smiling at me as I walked up. She didn't recognize me. Her smile fell quickly when she realized it was me.

"Adam!" The door to the pick-up was pulled closed. I pulled my arm back and without any more thought than that and I threw the fucking potato. It hit the center of his windshield as he tried to start the pick-up. He was apparently nervous because in the process of trying to start it, he gave it too much gas and flooded it. I slammed my hand against the window,

SCOOTINAMERICA-INSIDE MY HELMET

"Open up!" He wouldn't look at me; he just kept staring at the steering wheel cranking the engine. Laura was still standing there but I ignored her for now as I continued to beat on the driver's side window. "Open the fucking door" He cranked it over again and the third time was a charm. I literally had to jump out of the way as the chicken-shit raced out of the parking lot. Once he was gone, that was when I looked at my wife.

"It's not what you think," she said with tears flowing freely down her pretty face. I had my answer about whether or not she'd lie about it if I hadn't caught her.

I was suddenly exhausted. "If he is what you want then go get him." I walked away too angry and hurt to talk. I had to get out of there. I had to get home. I kept telling myself that things wouldn't look so bleak in the light of day.

I was wrong. I woke up later that morning and indeed she had not come home and had to remind myself of what I'd seen and that my marriage was over. I had left Ft. Myers a few days ago feeling like change was going to take place in our lives when I got back. I guess I was at least right about that.

SCOOTINAMERICA-INSIDE MY HELMET

Traveling is never easy. This photo was taken from the road prior to the night's event

CHAPTER FOUR

"If you did not serve in your military, find time to serve those who did."—Adam Sandoval

November 10, 2014

My mind was buzzing and my limbs were so charged up with adrenaline that they tingled. Normal thoughts and emotions were banished for the moment. I was happy, but that happiness was also tinged with an underlying sense of anxiety; the anxiety that almost always comes with starting something new. This day was the culmination of a lifetime of dreams and months of hard work and preparation. It was going to be the day that I embarked on a journey that would reshape the man I had become into the man I always wanted to be. Scooter was with me of course and so was a film crew from Big Block. The place was Six Bends Harley Davidson, Scott Fischer Enterprises' newest venture and a Harley enthusiasts dream. I found it fitting that it would be the place where I would finally kick off mine.

The past six months had been a journey of sorts for me leading up to the one I was beginning today. I had to re-learn how to be a single man, something I had thought I would never be again. I couldn't pinpoint the exact day, time or month that mine and Laura's relationship began to decline…but I can pinpoint the exact day when I accepted that it was over and I had to move on. Surprisingly, the night I found out she cheated on me wasn't it. Without a doubt that's where it began for me. I filed for divorce and went through the motions of what I had to do…but my heart wasn't in any of it. My heart still wanted Laura and it battled with my head constantly. The day that my head and my heart finally came to an agreement came in the form of meeting Laura at a restaurant to hash out some of the details of our divorce. Honestly to this day I don't remember all of the specifics of that conversation. I'm sure it's because there was one thing she said that I couldn't forget. Learning that you've been betrayed in a physical

SCOOTINAMERICA-INSIDE MY HELMET

sense is painful, but I didn't realize until that moment that emotional infidelity cut even deeper.

At some point during our conversation she simply said, "We talked about it Adam and we decided that if you see him around town and you try to do anything to him, he'll just lay down and let you put the beating to him…and then we'll call the police." It was one of those things that you wish you had heard wrong. It wasn't bad enough that this man had slept with my wife and refused to even look me in the eye when he got caught, but now she was worried about him and she felt some kind of need to "protect" him from me.

I walked out of there that day with the resolution to move on with my life and I did…eventually. For about six months after my divorce…in which the judge awarded me practically everything…I reverted to my old ways. I worked hard and partied even harder once again…until one night I had another epiphany. I'd gone to a local bar and at the end of the night as I'd done before; I invited a bunch of "friends" back to my house to finish the party. We were around the pool and the huge screen television that hung over it was on playing a music video and I was sitting next to it with a scantily clad girl in each arm and for some reason it hit me that none of these people were there because of me. They were just like the people I used to spend thousands on partying in Las Vegas after a big fight or renting limousines to take us to the fights and out to a club afterwards…they were there for the free booze and the big TV and the nice pool and the nice house, or whatever I happened to be offering that night. These two women cuddled up to me didn't even care that they were essentially "sharing" me. How could I expect people to respect me when I was spending time with people who had so little respect for themselves? I knew that my part of being with these people was about; it was me not wanting to be alone. I was going about this the wrong way and suddenly I knew that I had to make some changes. There had to be more to life than this. I actually went into my bathroom to be alone and sat there for a while just thinking about what I wanted to do with my life. The major decision I made that night was that this outrageous lifestyle was definitely not it.

SCOOTINAMERICA-INSIDE MY HELMET

With that in mind, I went back out to the party and shocked about a dozen people when I announced that the party was over and they had to go home.

The next week was spent doing some serious soul-searching. The idea of doing the ride came back to the forefront of my mind once again and took root. I could do this alone...me and Scooter. I actually started brainstorming ideas and trying to figure out how I could make this work. At the end of that week I flew to Wisconsin for the Fourth of July weekend and a family reunion. There was one more thing I needed before I committed to it.

My father Blaine is one of those blue collar guys who wore blue jeans and cowboy boots his entire life. He worked for everything he ever had and never expected handouts from anyone. Then one day at sixty years old, his entire life changed. He was involved in a car accident that would leave him in a wheelchair for the rest of his life. He was a quadriplegic and from one moment to the next he went from being the guy that took care of everything to the man who had no choice but to accept the help of those around him. If anyone knew about how quickly life could change...it was him.

As we sat there surrounded by family and loved ones I asked him if we could talk in private. He told me yes and we went out back. I told him, "I've been thinking a lot about what I want to do with my life lately. I am not sure that all of the "stuff" I've worked so hard to accumulate is the answer. It's just not making me happy. It's a temporary fix...but in the long run it's really like putting a Band-Aid on my unhappiness. I have this idea and I wanted to run it by you and see what you think."

"I'm listening."

"Laura and I talked a lot about doing a ride for charity...something for one of the military charities. We had an idea that would involve us riding the bikes across the United States, raising money as we went. When we were together I thought about ways to market it as a "couple's thing" so I had kind of tucked it

SCOOTINAMERICA-INSIDE MY HELMET

away for a while when we first split up. Lately though I've been thinking seriously about it again."

"What about financing it, and work?"

"I'm brainstorming ways to market this and get sponsors…but honestly Dad, I'm thinking about just selling everything and taking off. Maybe I'll get the sponsors and maybe I won't…but one of the things Laura said to me in the midst of the divorce that really stuck with me was, *"All you care about is money."* I wondered if she was just being mean, or if she really believed that. Then I wondered if she believed that because I'd put too much emphasis on it all along and I wondered if it was what other people saw when they looked at me as well. I took a good look around at all of the things I had and realized that if they were gone…I'd still be me." The realization that comfort doesn't bring peace was setting in for me, but I still wasn't certain how to describe it. "The bottom line, Dad is that I want to do something for someone else. I want to do something that matters. It may be too late to serve in the military, but maybe I can do something else to give back. Maybe I can serve right here at home."

My Dad looked at me and I'm not sure what I expected him to say…I am sure that it wasn't what came out of his mouth. "Go do it, Adam. If you don't, you're an idiot." That was it. In the simplest terms possible my father had summed it up. I had the opportunity to live a dream and if I let it pass me by I was an idiot, plain and simple. Four months later I was here at the starting line.

**My step-mother Jackie and my father Blaine who is
now ScootinAmerica's Campaign Manager**

CHAPTER FIVE

"There is a certain enthusiasm in liberty that makes human nature rise above itself, in acts of bravery and heroism."—Alexander Hamilton

I sold my house and all of my possessions over the course of a couple of months. Towards the end, about three weeks before I left I loaded up a trailer that I had with art and motorcycle parts…and all kinds of other things. It was everything I had left. Everything I couldn't or didn't want to sell on Craigslist or to friends, and it was a lot. It was thousands of dollars in stuff. It was stuff that I think I just needed to prove to myself that I didn't need. I had to prove that none of it defined me. I took it to the swap meet and I drove around until I came up on this older man who seemed like he did this for a living. I showed him what I had and said,

"I'm selling it all, the trailer too. I need to get rid of it now. How much will you give me for it?"

The man looked it over and said, "How much do you want?" I could tell by the look on his face that he didn't think he would be able to afford what I was asking.

"Five hundred dollars?"

"For everything?"

"Yep, for everything including the trailer." The man couldn't pay me fast enough then and I drove away happier than he was. I was liberated of all of the things I'd spent my life accumulating. Now I sat ready to begin the next chapter of my life, not with regret for the things I lost but with a sense of freedom for the things I was about to gain.

SCOOTINAMERICA-INSIDE MY HELMET

I had a plan at that point that involved visiting every Harley Davidson dealership in the lower 48 states…696 stops in 365 days. The trip would break three world records and hopefully raise a ton of money and awareness for the children of fallen soldiers and veterans. The charity I'd chosen was the American Legion Legacy Scholarship Fund and thanks to some great people like my friend Erin who helped me with the logo, my dreams began turning into realities. There were some people that weren't so helpful or happy for me like the man I formerly worked with who tried to steal the idea and the logo that Erin helped me design. That was a whole other nightmare but after going through the end of my marriage I'd have to say in the scheme of things it was a blip. We got through it and by Veteran's Day 2014, we were ready to kick this thing off.

Leading up to the day we left I had marketed the trip not only as a charity ride, but as a ride to bring people of a common interest together. I wanted people to think of it along the lines of when "Forrest Gump" ran and people joined him. The day I took off my sister and her boyfriend and about five other good friends showed up to ride with us for the first leg of the journey. I'd been expecting them…but I have to say I was surprised when a guy that I'd met at a bike rally months earlier showed up as well. While at the rally he was going to sleep under a tree, so my crew invited him inside our hotel room. My friend Tony said, *"We are not going to just let You GI Joe it under a tree."* G.I. Joe is the name we gave to this guy. He was about twenty-five years old and told us he recently spent seven years in the Coast Guard. He has an innocent look about him until you look into his dark eyes. That's where the evidence of everything he'd seen and been through in his young life was held. He had mentioned the day I met him that he would like to go along, but since then I hadn't heard a word from him, so I was definitely surprised.

He showed up dressed in blue jeans that looked like they'd seen better days and a black leather jacket. He wore a metal key on a chain around his neck and he had a pair of gloves and a thin gray beanie for his head. He was riding a Harley Sportster. It's a bike that was never meant to see weather or long trips. The tires,

SCOOTINAMERICA-INSIDE MY HELMET

suspension and the gas tank were both small and there was no
windshield. He had a small green duffel bag with him and that was
all he was carrying. It was the kind of bag that soldiers got used to
carrying everything in that they needed or that was dear to them
when they were away from home. He didn't have any chaps and no
heated gear. I honestly thought he'd just come to see us off until he
said,

"I want to go with you. I can ride with you for two
weeks."

I didn't want to discourage this guy. I was honored that he
was willing to dedicate two weeks of his life to our cause…but I
was genuinely worried about him. We were headed north and it
was very likely we were going to run into some serious weather and
scary road conditions.

"Man, I'd love to have you, I just don't think you're really
equipped for ten to fifteen degree weather and long stretches on
the road."

"I'll be alright," he said. "I need to do this." He didn't tell
me right then why it was he needed to do this, but it was a
sentiment I could identify with. This was something I needed to do
as well. I told myself he could ride along until he decided it was too
cold or too dangerous. I honestly didn't expect him to make it the
entire two weeks…but I had sorely underestimated him.

We left Ft. Meyers with a hell of a send-off and headed
north. It was warm at first but it was only getting colder and I had
chaps and a windshield. I didn't hear a single complaint out of G.I.
Joe though. I guess when you're used to the conditions our men
and women in military are presented with, the weather we
experienced and the discomfort of riding that little bike of his
sometimes six hundred or more miles in one day was a minor
thing. At each stop along the way he took pictures and ran the
video for me and collected money for us. With his close cropped
black hair and short beard and mustache coupled with his lean
muscular build, he actually resembled what G.I. Joe would look like

28

SCOOTINAMERICA-INSIDE MY HELMET

in real life in my head, and he turned out to be everything that I thought a soldier should be. The name my crew had given him stuck because it was so fitting and knowing him only reinforced the idea that I was doing this for all of the right reasons. He only gave me more reason for that respect as time went on.

Our second day on the road we stopped at Pensacola Harley Davidson. It was an extra significant stop for me because it was Veteran's Day, a day set aside to honor the very people I was doing this for. That day there was a gathering of what we refer to as "Pelican's." These are the older guys who hang out at the Harley Dealerships having coffee and shooting the shit. They were sitting outside around back and we sat with them and talked for a while. As we were sitting there another older guy pulled up on his bike. The men we were talking to were really surprised to see him. As he approached, they told us that this guy was a Vietnam Veteran and sometimes he didn't leave his house for weeks at a time. Most recently he'd been in self-imposed isolation for three weeks. He was tough looking and you could see in his body and his eyes that he'd seen more than a few battles over the years. He had that same haunted look that a lot of veteran's carry around…but his demeanor and voice were soft and friendly. The first thing he told me was,

"I heard on the radio that you were going to be here. I had to come out and see you and Scooter today. I think what you're doing is great. I wanted to play this song I wrote if it's okay? I call it called Thunder Child."

"Of course, that would be great," I told him. He played this CD for me and it brought a tear to my eye, thinking of all the struggles these men faced coming home from war. After the CD stopped I gave him a hug and told him honestly, "I loved it."

G.I. Joe and I talked with him for a while. Joe noticed while they were talking that the other man wore a P-32 on a chain around his neck. It was similar to the chain G.I. Joe carried his key on. He asked him about that and the man said,

29

SCOOTINAMERICA-INSIDE MY HELMET

"I was a Machine Gunner in the Army during Nam. We were fighting in the jungle and throughout this jungle there were these villages where women and kids lived. A lot of these kids were starving...they just didn't have enough food. The war had been going on for a long time in their country. I started trading things with the other soldiers...like smokes, for extra food rations. I'd take the rations down to the village and give them to the kids. This was what I used to open the rations for them and I've worn in on this chain ever since. It's a...reminder." He didn't say what it was a "reminder" of exactly, but it was easy to see as he spoke about those kids and how he'd gone without things to make sure they had food to eat...that the reminder might possibly be that even in the midst of war, humanity has to prevail.

G.I. Joe pulled the chain he wore the key on out of his shirt and he told the other man, "When I was in the Coast Guard my main job was apprehending human traffickers...coyotes. I used this key to open a Shipping container that had been dropped off on an island in the middle of the Pacific not long before I discharged. The container was full of human beings and they'd just dropped them off there...they were left to die inside that steel box."

Listening to these two men talk about the things that they'd done and seen in the pursuit of keeping all of us safe and free, gave me chills. At least four decades or maybe five, separated the two men but they were brothers in the sense that they had both been willing to give up all of the comforts that the rest of us enjoyed every day to make sure we had the freedom to enjoy those things. To a casual observer you might think they were free of the burdens of war...but it was something that they would both carry within themselves and around their necks forever. Before we left there that day, the older man asked if he could lead us to our next dealership. I told him we would be honored. He led us...fifteen to twenty bikes, onto our next stop. Before he left there to return to his home, he and G.I. Joe exchanged necklaces. For me it was one of those surreal moments that I knew I was blessed to be there to witness. It was one of the moments of this trip that I knew would stay with me forever.

SCOOTINAMERICA-INSIDE MY HELMET

The crew that rode with us for the first week or two. (Left to right) Clark, GI Joe, me, my sister Trisha, Paul and Kenny

CHAPTER SIX

**"If you're brave enough to say goodbye, life will reward you
with a new hello."— Paulo Coelho**

From Pensacola we continued heading north with stops in
Gainesville and Buell. Every day on the road was turning out to be
a new adventure, but as I rode along the roads and highways of our
beautiful country, I also had a lot going on inside my helmet. I had
been in negotiations before I left with a production company who
expressed interest in filming the ride. They called me not long
before I left and told me they were shopping networks and looking
for sponsors. They still wanted to do the show, but they wanted me
to wait for spring to leave on my trip. They talked about putting
money up front, but at this point they said they couldn't do that
until spring either. They needed time to put it all together. I was
disappointed, but far from devastated. The planning for this trip
had been done in detail with a lot of help from my father. After his
accident his greatest struggle was the thought of sitting around and
staring at the walls all day. Asking him to help me helped us both.
It gave him a new purpose in life and it took a lot of the pressure
off of me. But we'd both worked hard to make this happen in
November…not in the spring.

This ride had never been about getting on television for
me. This ride was about serving my country in the best way
possible with what I had. I told them that I would love for them to
do the show. It would certainly help to generate more
donations…more money for the kids. But, with or without a show,
I was ready to do this now. We talked a few more times and then a
week before I left they told me they were still interested and that
they would send a film crew for that day. Their crew ended up
being a no-show. I worked with a lot of film crews so I told them
I'd take care of it, and I did. I called a favor in to an old friend I
had done many shows with in the past. He jumped on it and got
the cameras and man out there, but no one from the production

SCOOTINAMERICA-INSIDE MY HELMET

company showed up that day. I wasn't so concerned about it that I was losing any sleep over it, but it was on my mind.

Also on my mind of course was Laura. This single life was new and although I had G.I. Joe and a lot of friends and support along the way, I wasn't used to being alone. She still reached out to me once or twice a week with a text or a phone call. She was starting to express regret about the way we'd ended things and each time I had a conversation or got a text from her, it messed with my head. I often wondered: *Did I cut her off too soon? Did I give enough?* But each time it came down to the reality that she was with him..... And still texting me. I had to keep telling myself those are not the values that I'm looking for in life.

My social media following was picking up and a lot of the time my thoughts were on that. I always had to think about how to market this trip and how to generate more interest and more sponsors. I didn't know from one day to the next where we would sleep, so of course that was always on my mind. For the most part we camped wherever we could find a safe place off the side of the road or we stayed with supporters along the way that were generous enough to offer us shelter for the night. Scooter was a trooper as usual. He loves to ride and he's always ready to roll with the punches. I made sure he had a warm place to ride and sleep and plenty of food in his belly and he was a happy guy. He was easy, but planning it all from one day to the next in my head was stressful at times. The money I'd earned from selling my things had to last for an entire year on the road so I needed to make wise decisions that didn't include hotels and big, expensive meals. I didn't want to use any of the donated money. The plan was to donate all of that to the American Legion. It was for the kids, that's what this was all about and I wasn't willing to spend any of the money that was intended for them on our operations budget. I do know that's how charity works and if I ever wanted to do it full time that is how I would need to operate. I understand that charities need money to operate and accomplish their goals, but for this year I wanted to do it my way.

SCOOTINAMERICA-INSIDE MY HELMET

So as we rode, these things were all present in my mind. But not so much that I didn't realize how fortunate I was to see so many beautiful sights and meet so many interesting, good-hearted people. I was also enjoying all of the activities we were being invited to participate in such as a Cruise-In in Tallahassee and Toys for Tots rally in Fortwalton Beach. The trip wasn't designed to be easy, and that was okay. We were raising money for a great cause and I was living my dream and I couldn't really ask for more than that.

Before we made it out of Florida I got a call from the producers of Animal Planet's Pit Bulls and Parolees. They were doing a ride for one of the regulars on the show, Earl Moffett. He was one of the first parolee's that became a part of the cast. He suffered an injury in 2006 playing contact football in prison. His cervical nerve root was injured and he lost the use of his right arm. They were raising money for his medical care and they were calling to invite Scooter and me to lead the ride! I was really excited about that as we headed into Louisiana…but at the same time my heart was heavy. New Orleans would be the end of the ride for my road brother G.I. Joe. He'd be heading back to Florida to have Thanksgiving dinner with his Grandmother. It was his first Thanksgiving home in seven years so I was happy for him…but I was definitely going to miss his presence.

We met more incredible people and raised more money as we went through Mississippi. Every night was spent looking for a warm place to lay our heads, and we were amazed at how many people generously opened up their homes for us. We also got an awesome escort to the Louisiana border and along the way we got to see a lot of beautiful sights. One of the landmarks we got to visit was The Friendship Tree. It's a five hundred year old oak tree that sits on the Southern Miss Gulf Park campus in Long Beach, Mississippi. It has survived countless floods and hurricanes during its five centuries of life, including Katrina that hit that region hard. As we made our way into and through Louisiana, we were treated to some good old southern hospitality. They fed us until we were ready to pop and I got my first taste of real, homemade Cajun goodness like boudin. For those of you who have never had the

SCOOTINAMERICA-INSIDE MY HELMET

pleasure, boudin is sausage made from a pork rice dressing and stuffed into pork casings. It was definitely one of my most memorable meals and a must have next time I pass through that neck of the woods.

We rolled into New Orleans on November twenty-first. I just have to say, what a great place New Orleans is. Every street in the French Quarter offers something different from the last. The architecture is incredible and the atmosphere itself is intoxicating. From food to music to drinks and street performers, it's a place that has something for everyone.

That first night in New Orleans was mostly about relaxing. G.I. Joe and I opened up a bottle of whiskey and I got to know him better that evening and by the time it was over I would finally understand why this trip was so important to him. We started out just talking about everything, he told me more about his job in the Coast Guard. As he talked about the things the Coast Guard does, things like search and rescue and chasing down drug traffickers and human coyotes, I tried to imagine being so young and so far away from home while seeing and enduring the things that this young man did. I didn't know him before he went in, but from the age of eighteen to twenty-five he'd dealt with so much that from what I saw today I had no doubt that he may have left a boy, but he absolutely returned a man. I hadn't heard the worst of it yet though. That night as we talked Joe told me about coming home to his father's house after getting out of the service.

I could tell that there was something really troubling that he wanted to share…or maybe he wasn't sure if he wanted to share it or not? Finally he simply said,

"About a week after I got home, my dad killed himself. I found his body." I didn't know what to say to that, but in all honesty I don't think he expected me to say anything. He just needed me to be a friend and listen. He took out a picture of his dad and showed it to me. He was a big Latin guy with a lot of muscle. "He was a pro body-builder," G.I. told me. "It's where I got my passion for fitness." He was silent again for a second and

SCOOTINAMERICA-INSIDE MY HELMET

then he said, "He's been battling demons for a long time." That was all he seemed to want to say. I didn't ask any questions, I just gave him a hug and that seemed to be all he needed. I was touched that he would share something so deeply personal with me and it gave me an even deeper understanding of what he'd been through and what he'd needed a break from. We all need a break sometimes, a shoulder to lean on and an ear to listen…and then the strong ones like G.I. Joe saddle back up and keep moving forward.

                    ****

The next day we had an event at Wet and Wild Saloon in Houma, about an hour drive out of New Orleans. It was fundraiser being held in honor of a local biker who had undergone transplant surgery as well as a friend of his in a similar circumstance. It was one of those things that the biker community is great at…coming together for a cause. Scooter and I were honored to be asked to appear at this event and for the opportunity to help out with another great cause.

That night G.I. Joe, Scooter and I were treated to a special surprise. The executives of Pit Bulls and Parolees put us up in an Executive Suite and we were invited to a barbecue and party to kick off the ride for Earl that would happen the next morning. G.I. Joe's departure had been on my mind a lot and I was hoping that I could do or say something to let him know how much I appreciated his friendship and all the help he'd given us on the road. I talked to the producers of the show and I asked if G.I. Joe could lead the ride with us. They didn't go for it. They were televising this and he was an "unknown" in their eyes and the eyes of the viewers. It was disappointing to me, but understandable from their perspective, but I was not going to let that be the end of it.

That night we found a party. It was held by Bacardi Rum and it was in the French Quarter in a system of old warehouse type buildings that were all inter-connected. It was an invitation only thing, but thousands of people had been invited and had shown up.

SCOOTINAMERICA-INSIDE MY HELMET

Many of them were decked out in capes and masks and feathers…full masquerade and ready to party NOLA style. Besides being a great party, the people watching opportunities were endless and there were several bird handlers there as well with gorgeous owls and ravens. It was a perfect lead-in to the ride the next day.

We met at Villabos Rescue Center, the heart and soul of the reality show. The center serves an endless flow of stray and unwanted pit bulls and it's staffed with incredible people that in spite of some bad choices they may have made in their past, they're working towards a brighter future by reaching out to help others. Right before the ride I took the producer aside again and explained a bit more in depth about GI Joe. I told him how much it meant to me to have him lead this ride by my side. He understood and gave me the green light. When GI Joe pulled up I was excited to tell him he would be leading this ride by my side on national television. I think it meant a lot to him, and frankly it may have meant more to me. This was an awesome experience. The streets were blocked off for the ride and a ton of people showed up to ride along, donate and show their support. We were led by a full police escort from Claiborne Ave. to the Tahyo Tavern where we were served one hell of a delicious potluck lunch all arranged by the producers of Pit Bulls and Parolees. It was another memorable experience for a great cause that I have the pleasure of saying I was allowed to be a part of.

The next day as I said good-bye to New Orleans, I also said good-bye to my brother G.I. Joe. As Scooter and I ride on, G.I. Joe will always be in our hearts and part of some of the greatest memories we've made on the road. I was sad to see him go, but thankful for the opportunity to call him my friend.

SCOOTINAMERICA-INSIDE MY HELMET

**GI Joe riding by my side on set of Animal Planet's Pit
bulls & Parolees**

CHAPTER SEVEN

"If you are grateful for everything, then whatever you have is enough."—J. Baadsgaard

One of the things that garnered a lot of concern from my friends and supporters when I began this ride was my bike. Most people didn't understand why I was choosing to ride this old bike on a trip that would take me tens of thousands of miles. It's hard to explain sentimental attachment...but that was the bottom line. I'd sold nearly everything before I left Florida because in the grand scheme, none of it mattered, it was all replaceable, and it had no sentimental value. But this bike was different. I was attached to it and I had faith in it and I still do...all of these miles later.

I had more than one person ask me why I didn't at the very least replace my exhaust. It was old and rusty with scars and bruises from the many trips I'd taken it on. It was covered with snake trail patches from being welded back together each time that it broke. Every scar has a story of some kind behind it and that's not just true for the human kind. There were tons of memorable stories behind those scars and I felt like getting rid of the exhaust would be like being unfaithful to those memories. The patches gave it character and I loved it.

As Scooter and I made our way into Texas the exhaust started giving me trouble. It was patched back together a couple of times between Louisiana and Texas but after hitting our first three or four dealerships and finally making it to the first dealership in Houston, the War Horse decided to act up. We were at Mancuso Harley-Davidson and there was a good turn-out of well-wishers and people who followed us online. We had a great time...and then as I went to leave and everyone was gathered around to see us off, I started up the bike and the exhaust fell off...right there in the parking lot. The embarrassment of that was nothing compared to the frustration that would come later. The dealership that I was at

SCOOTINAMERICA-INSIDE MY HELMET

didn't have the parts I needed. It was an old bike and many dealers don't carry parts for those older years. They are more focused on the new bikes and that's what they see on a daily basis. If they ordered them, it was going to be Saturday before they came in and that would put us way behind. The other store wouldn't be open two days so it looked like we were grounded in Houston for at least one more day and the weather was turning nasty. I patched the exhaust as well as I could for the night by wrapping it with thin, tiny band wire before we left the dealer. From there we rode in the wind and the cold to a place that some kind people on social media had told me about. It was called the Hawg Stop. The Hawg Stop is a bar and grille and "open air" biker hangout owned by a guy named Delmer Barkley. Besides the bar which is a famous biker hang-out with live music nearly every night, there's a campground as well. When Scooter and I got there, the owner came out to meet us himself. After we were introduced he asked,

"You're having some troubles with your bike?"

"Yeah, I've been patching up this old exhaust for a long time, but it looks like I'm going to have to give in and just put a new one on it. I have to wait two days for the dealership to open."

"Well, while you're here, make yourself at home and it's all on the house."

"Wow, that's incredible, thank you."

"I respect what you're doing and I'm glad I'm in a position to help you out here."

I thanked him profusely and once we had our campsite set up we went over to the bar. They supplied us with a delicious hamburger dinner and all the whiskey I was interested in drinking. While I ate I struck up a conversation with some of the other bikers in the bar. These guys were local "Oil Riggers." They were hard-working, hard-playing motorcycle enthusiasts and really interesting to talk to. I told them who Scooter and I were and what we were doing. Before the night was over I ended up challenging

SCOOTINAMERICA-INSIDE MY HELMET

some of these guys to a push-up contest. I got paid for every push-up I could do beyond each one of theirs. By the night's end I had raised another two-hundred dollars for the kids and I'd had a great time doing it.

When we left the campground it was even colder then when we arrived and now it was raining. We made the long ride back into town to the dealership and they told me,

"We can still fix it, but you'll have to leave it here for the night. The parts won't be in until the am"

That meant one more night in Houston and one more day behind. I was frustrated again, but still trying not to let it get me down. Before I began this trip and for the past two weeks I'd been on the road I had considered as most people might, the possibility of something happening to me. Biker's die every day on the roads and although it wasn't something I focused on or obsessed over, it was definitely a consideration. At one point I had even talked to my dad about it.

"I keep thinking, what if something happens out here? What if I get in an accident on the road?"

"You can't think like that son. That kind of thinking holds you back and causes you to miss out on so many things."

"How do I not worry about it though? I'll be alone and so far from home. I'll be out in all kinds of weather and with all kinds of hazards on the roads."

My dad said the perfect thing then to make me understand that I was catastrophizing a situation that hadn't even happened yet. "Adam I was two miles from home in an F-250 when I had my accident and you know what that proves to me?"

"What's that?"

SCOOTINAMERICA-INSIDE MY HELMET

"It can happen anytime and anywhere, touring the country or sitting on the couch. When it's your time it just is…and there's nothing you can do about it. Worrying won't help; it will only hold you back."

I held those words with me on days like this one especially. I left the bike because I had no choice and I got on my Facebook page and I put out a message to my friends and followers that said,

"Hey guys, the bike is broke down and we're stuck in Houston for another night and looking for a place to stay. If anyone can help us out, I'd be so grateful."

It wasn't long before I got a message back from a woman who simply said, "I have a place you can stay."

"Great!" I told her where we were and she said,

"I'll be there soon to pick you up."

I was sitting outside waiting for her, happy and feeling lucky that there were so many kind people willing to help us…at first. Then for some reason little doubts started to seep into my consciousness and that unnecessary worry that my dad had warned me about began to take root. I went to her Facebook page and what I saw only caused the dark thoughts in my head to escalate. The photos on her Facebook were few…only three that I could see. But what was in them fed thoughts that I'd had before and made them fester while I sat there. The photos were of what I could only assume was this lady in a turban and camels in the desert. Next I started to google her name, and nothing…I could not find one thing on her. One thing besides the possibility of an accident that I had considered on the backside of this trip was the possibility of drawing negative attention since what I was doing was for the military. What if I somehow became a target for one of the branches of terrorism that our military fights every day? My head began spinning thoughts off of that and by the time she pulled up in her beat-up Chevy pick-up I wasn't sure that I should

SCOOTINAMERICA-INSIDE MY HELMET

get in. She rolled down the window as I walked over to the truck and she smiled. The first thing she said to me was,

"Don't worry, you're safe." I know that was meant to put me at ease. Maybe she could see the anxiety or the uncertainty in my face. Either way, it only made me more suspicious. I asked myself, *"Why would she say that right off the bat?"* Again, I'm not sure if she could see it in my face or my body language, but sensing I wasn't comfortable. Before she arrived I found a local bar so I told her it was a long day and asked if she would join me for a beer. I figured this would give me more time to evaluate the situation and see if I wanted to accept her offer of a place to stay or not. She agreed to go and have a drink with me and while we sat in this little bar full of locals she told me her back story…and I had been way off base. This lady as it turned out was a member of the local militia. She also had a high clearance grade with the military which made her a "Ghost" and that was why her Facebook photos were what they were. We talked for quite a while and I decided pretty quickly to take her up on her offer of a place to stay. That night she made us dinner and in the morning she made us breakfast. Talking to her and spending time in her home turned out to actually be a wonderful experience that I was glad I hadn't let my fear hold me back from. It was another memory that I could commit to the idea forming in my head since the first day of this trip, "People are really good at heart."

I left Houston with more lessons learned about the innate kindness of the average soul and headed to Dallas/Ft. Worth. Not long before we made it there another setback was in store for me. The Warhorse started losing oil. I drove as fast as I could to the nearest KOA campground and I called the dealership, but they were closed for the holiday. It was the day before Thanksgiving, Friday was the soonest they'd be open. Once more it looked like we were stranded for a couple of days. We camped that night and I woke up the next morning thinking about the holiday. It's funny, but never in my adult life had Thanksgiving or Christmas held any real, significant meaning for me. I even had a tendency to look at them as another excuse people used not go to work. This was a problem I have experienced with every relationship I ever had, I

SCOOTINAMERICA-INSIDE MY HELMET

was a classic workaholic and not even a holiday was reason enough to focus on anything other than work. I can remember countless Thanksgivings where I didn't want to go do the big party, fighting with my spouse about all the things I would rather be doing. But that morning as Scooter and I sat alone at that campground and I thought of all of the people home having dinner and just hanging out with their friends and family I was overwhelmed by a sense of loneliness that exceeded any I'd felt so far. For the first time in my life I wanted the traditions. It's funny how sometimes we can see life so much more clearly when we are having a hard time. Maybe this was exactly what I needed, maybe this trip is going to teach me much more then humility. The weather was cold and gray and maybe that also had something to do with the melancholy mood I was in. I definitely wasn't feeling up to "giving thanks" as I tucked Scooter into my jacket and we walked the several miles to a little bar up the road to get something to eat.

The place wasn't packed but there were enough people there that as we sat and ate free bar food and talked, the loneliness began to ebb away a little. I met a really nice couple and they offered us a warm place to stay in their home that night. The next day they gave me a ride down to the dealership and I was informed they had the parts in stock but they also told me they wouldn't work on my bike because, "It was too old." My new friends were kind enough to let me pick up the parts and use their garage to put the bike back together. We sat there all afternoon tearing that engine apart and fixing it while drinking down some beer until atlas the "Warhorse" was alive again. Accidentally it seemed, I'd found something new to be thankful for after all.

Me and the team from Mancuso showing off my new exhaust

CHAPTER EIGHT

"No one would have crossed the ocean if he could have gotten off the ship in the storm." –Charles Kettering

As we made our way deeper into Texas Mother Nature continued to rage. The stretches of road in the great state of Texas are longer than most other states and it afforded me maybe too much time for the thoughts inside my helmet. The foremost one at that time was keeping Scooter and I warm. As we neared Brownsville we had been on the road for hours and it was late and raining and I was wet and literally freezing. The biting cold had spread painfully through my entire body and it only added to the exhaustion that was weighing me down.

I had been doing my best to be frugal with the little money I had to finance the trip. It had to last for at least a year and although my friends at Scott Fischer Enterprises were putting up most of the money for my gas, the rest was on me. I hadn't paid for a hotel room so far but I had reached that point of exhaustion where it just wouldn't be safe to go on any further. I looked for a motel that might be inexpensive and I found one just off the highway that said it had rooms for $29.00 per night.

The outside of the place was run-down. It looked like one of those where people paid for rooms by the hour. Weeds grew up through the cracks in the concrete path and the litter from cheap take-out meals lay strewn across it. The external stairs that led up to a second floor were wooden and looked weather beaten…but I didn't care about any of that. All I needed was a clean, dry place to rest my head for the night. I paid for the room and realized too late that the building inspector was either paid-off or drunk on the job if this place had passed any kind of inspection. As soon as I opened the door I was assaulted with the sights and smells of everything that had been there before me. Flipping on the light, I suddenly felt as if I was trapped in a horror film. It was cramped and dim…but

SCOOTINAMERICA-INSIDE MY HELMET

that wasn't what worried me. The walls were stained with something black. I suppose it could have been decades of filth, but it looked suspiciously like old blood that had been smeared all over it. There was no way to tell what color the thin and worn carpeting had been before the build-up of funk began and the linens on the bed were just as questionable. I am not what one would call the prissy type. I have lived in many rough apartments and stayed in many substandard rooms. I have even slept next to dumpsters a time or two on this trip. But when it came to this room it was too much for even the most road hardened bikers so I immediately left and went back up to the lobby. The night clerk looked like he was used to people returning right away and as soon as I said,

"I can't sleep in that room. It's just not healthy."

His reply was, "Okay, but we don't do refunds."

I just left without saying anything to him. At that point I was so far beyond exhausted and frustrated he and I were both better off for it. I went back to the horror room and checked out the rest of it. The bathroom had the same dark stains on the walls and the shower and the little window that faced out to the parking lot was surrounded with little patches of mold. There was just no way I could imagine sleeping here. I went back outside. It wasn't getting any warmer or any earlier so I had to make a decision right away. I looked at the window again and suddenly had an idea. Luckily I was on the first floor so I pulled the bike up as close to the window as I could and then I pulled off my waterproof tarp. I stripped down outside the door, taking everything off until I stood butt naked and I wrapped up in the tarp. I left the clothes I was wearing with my stuff on the bike and went back inside. I opened up the window so that if anyone messed with the bike at all, I could hear it, and then I lay down on the floor in the plastic tarp with Scooter cuddled against me and we went to sleep.

I woke up when the sun came up in the morning and I used the hottest water I could stand and took a shower in the nasty stall. I wrapped back up in the tarp and dropped it before I stepped outside, leaving it behind in the room. I got dressed and I got the

SCOOTINAMERICA-INSIDE MY HELMET

hell out of there praying I hadn't taken anything that was lurking in there with me.

       ****

In spite of the hiccups like the motel and the weather along the way, Scooter and I sent our first check to the American Legion Scholarship fund ten days before we reached the one month mark on our journey. It totaled over four thousand dollars and it gave me a great sense of pride to be able to send it. As much fun as I was having and as much as I was enjoying my new experiences and making new friends, sending that check reinforced the idea that even when things got rough, I was doing the right thing. It further cemented the idea that we as American's could come together and really make a difference in the lives of those who were so willing to dedicate theirs to us.

As we continued our ride through the largest state in America stopping at over fifty dealerships the weather continued to worsen. It was cold, wet, icy and just plain miserable some days. Although I was determined not to let it stop us, it did slow us down at times. But, in the midst of the weather and all of these stops we were lucky enough to be invited to take part in more than one community event that brought us closer to the locals and once more helped us to define our mission. We took part in Toys for Tots rally in Corpus Christie and we did two more newspaper interviews along the way. We had a really nice dinner with some great guys from the American Legion Post 133 as well.

The bike had an issue with its wiring in Harker Heights and the guys at the Fort Hood dealership there fixed it for me at no cost. Then I moved on to Temple Texas to a store called Horny Toad HD. There I experienced another one of those emotional moments that would stick with me for a long time. A guy named George Lee who was Navy Veteran and a super nice guy. He and his crew gave us a really warm welcome and then George presented me with a star that was cut from an American flag.

SCOOTINAMERICA-INSIDE MY HELMET

"It's to thank you for your service to our nation," he told me.

Confused I said, "Service to my nation? I am doing this because I never served." Honestly at that point, the only things I felt I was servicing were my regrets.

"I disagree. What you're doing now out here on the road is service. I'm proud of you and even though you didn't go overseas…you're a brother of mine in every way possible."

I was choked up. This was the kind of acceptance that I have always dreamed about, to be a part of the bond that these soldiers carry together. Although it may not be exactly the same, it was an honor nonetheless to be at least experience a part of what these men and women share. I'm still at a loss for the words to adequately describe how it made me feel to know that this man that I looked up to and respected for all of the things he'd done for his country…was showing the same kind of respect for me. Even the smile that I had on my face didn't adequately reflect what I was feeling on the inside.

****

Throughout all of this, Christmas was rapidly approaching. My friends and followers on Facebook had taken to asking me what I wanted for Christmas. I realized that I didn't have to really even give that any thought. I knew what I wanted. I wanted people to help me spread the word about what we were doing for these kids so that in the years to come the money we are raising will be enough to make a significant impact on the lives of those who had lost so much. They have suffered indescribable pain in their young lives. The devastation of losing a parent is far-reaching and when these children begin to embark on their lives as adults, my wish is that they will be able to do that armed with the pride that can only come from being a part of a family who gave everything they had to protect and defend their country…and an education so that their boundaries may be limitless. I didn't have a budget for marketing. Social media and articles like the ones that some of the local media

SCOOTINAMERICA-INSIDE MY HELMET

have done for us is our only way to spread the word and solicit more support for this great cause. My Christmas wish was simply for more people to help me share this message along the way.

None of that is to say I wasn't feeling lonely. It was Christmas time and everywhere I looked I saw families celebrating their own traditions and just enjoying the privilege of being together during the holidays. Laura had still been texting me.

I would wake up in the morning sometimes with a text that would simply be a link to the country love song we danced to at our wedding, and other times it would just be a random love song. I didn't always respond to them…sometimes I just wasn't sure what she wanted me to say. I was sure she was trying desperately to keep my mind on her and to get me to give her back the attention I used to shower her with. It was always enough to get me to question myself again. Did I make the right decision about the divorce? Should I take her back? Although my brain knew that I was finally doing the right thing, my heart spiked with each message, especially as we rolled into the holidays.

I remember waking up one morning to a text that said, "I've been following the ride on Facebook. It sounds like you're having a great time. I should be out there with you. If I were there we could celebrate Christmas together. I still love you, Adam." That one hit me hard. I was already feeling the loneliness and it sounded like she was too. I text her back that time and said,

"I hope you have a good Christmas, Laura. I hope you know that I don't hate you and I have always hoped that we could stay friends through all of this."

"I can't be your friend," was her response to that.

It was times like that when I had to remind myself that my dream was now different from hers. I dream of a Christmas someday with a loved one who stood beside me in the hard times along with the good. I dream of one where I can indulge in old and customary traditions while forging out new ones that we create

SCOOTINAMERICA-INSIDE MY HELMET

together. Alone out here on the road sometimes it seems as though the thought of finding anyone to share this with might be impossible. For now dealing with loneliness would be part of my life and I'd have to find new ways to stave it away, but taking steps backwards was not the answer.

I chased away loneliness somedays with a simple look at my Facebook. Sometimes that was all I needed to remind myself of all of the kind and generous people that were pulling for me not just today, but every day that Scooter and I were on the road. The donations were coming in at most of the dealerships, my followers were multiplying, the word was getting out and I had faith that my Christmas wish would eventually come true. I spent my Christmas day reflecting on that as well as on the fact that being hundreds or thousands away from my own family had done nothing to weaken the bond that I had with them. That thought was only reinforced by this poem my mother wrote and sent to me for Christmas:

Who Hears Their Cries?

Just a man who heard the call

To help fallen soldiers one and all

With his little pup right by his side

Then others joined their noble ride.

Day by day his passion grew

Day by day the soldiers knew

Someone cared enough to give.

A year of his life he'll be put to test

As those fallen soldiers are laid to rest

Their families will know he hears their cries.

51

SCOOTINAMERICA-INSIDE MY HELMET

The Harley's they roll one by one

A mission accomplished when day is done.

His heart is big

The journey long

With our country's support

He won't go wrong.

The soldiers have fought

The soldiers have died

Their families have lost

Who hears their cries?

****

I made it through the holiday, and just about a week after Christmas it was so cold that the rain had turned to ice and it was hammering Texas. The whole state was under the siege of a rare, horrible storm. Everything was frozen solid. Icicles hung from bridges and black ice lay precariously in wait on the highway. Everyone was telling me that I had to stop and wait it out, that there was no way I could keep going. All I could think about was how much several days or a week of lodging was going to cost and how far behind it would put us in our tight schedule.

The temperature was just about six degrees above zero as we headed out from Legacy HD in Midland Texas with forty-five mph winds blowing right in my face. Midland was not only one of my favorite stops because of the great people…but it was our largest contributor to date at that time. We left Legend Harley Davidson with over two-thousand dollars in donations…and that was a nice thought to keep me warm on the inside at least. On the

SCOOTINAMERICA-INSIDE MY HELMET

outside…I was just plain freezing. My face shield had broken and I didn't have any heated gear. I had to hold the bike at a forty-five degree angle to keep the wind from blowing us over and Scooter had to ride inside my jacket as I desperately tried to keep him warm. The landscape around me was bare which somehow made it seem even colder. There were no homes or towns for miles on end. It was high desert, oil land and there was nowhere to pull over to even escape the cold for a few seconds between towns. I was left with literally no choice but to keep riding into this evil cold. It was about seventy or eighty miles between towns when I finally saw this little mini-mart/gas station and pulled into it. I stopped near the gas pumps and as I tried to take off my gas cap I realized my fingers were too frozen to work. I went inside, just hoping to thaw out just a little and the first thing my eyes landed on was one of those hot dog warmers with about six hot dogs inside of it. I stuck my hands underneath the sweet warmth of the light and the lady behind the counter freaked out.

"You can't put your hands in there!"

"I'm sorry, but they're so cold and numb I can't even unscrew my gas cap."

"It's a health hazard, you can't do that."

"How much are the hot dogs?" I asked her.

"Two dollars."

I counted them, there were six. I gave her the twelve bucks and then as I took my hotdogs out I defrosted my hands…just a little bit.

I left there and for the next forty or fifty miles there was nothing. There was no shelter anywhere and I was practically sucking face with my gas cap so I could stay behind the windshield as I did over a hundred miles per hour just trying to get somewhere warm and fast. If I have a guardian angel, he was shaking his head that day. When I pulled into the next gas station the woman

SCOOTINAMERICA-INSIDE MY HELMET

working there looked at me as soon as I walked in the door and said,

"Come in here and sit down. What are you doing out in this weather?" I sat down and as I warmed up I told her what we were doing. "Oh my goodness, you can't keep going in this weather. There's a hotel up the road. Let me get you a room where you can warm up and stay the night."

"No, I'm supposed to be at my next dealership in less than an hour. I have to keep going."

"Hon it's not safe out there."

"I'll be alright. I just need to warm up for a while if that's okay. If I could just sit here for a while until I thaw out."

"Of course you can." I sat and talked to this lady and Scooter and I started to warm up. It felt like my fingers were being stabbed with a thousand needles as they started to warm up. I hated to think that I would have to go back out in this cold. I again reminded myself as I often do that we have soldiers going to war missing limbs and I'm just lucky to be in the safety of my own country and that I still have my own limbs with which to feel the pain. It was with that in mind that we finally headed back out into the storm as the lady continued trying to talk me into letting her get me a room. I was grateful to her for the offer and the sentiment, but I was determined to keep going. By the time we reached the next dealership we were almost two hours late…but we had made it, alive.

**That day was so cold I saw no shame in sticking my
hand inside the hotdog warmer**

CHAPTER NINE

"We don't meet people by accident. They are meant to cross our path for a reason."—Unknown

I wouldn't have believed it possible, but the weather continued to worsen. Water that had once run beautifully through rivers and streams was now trapped in frozen chunks of ice and as solid as the frozen ground. The air was unnaturally cold and the chill breeze sliced through the protective layers that I wore. Icicles dangled from the trees like shadowy skeletons with long, reaching fingers and worst of all for a man and a dog on two wheels was the black ice that lay invisibly against the road like the welcome mat of death. Everywhere we stopped people told me that I couldn't keep going in this storm. I'm not sure if it was my determination to keep to my schedule, or just plain stubbornness, but I didn't want to hear it.

We'd made it to Fort Worth Harley Davidson when I got a call from my dad who had heard about the ice storm. "What's it like out there?"

"It's ugly, Dad. Cold, gray and everything is frozen including the roads."

"You need to stay put until it clears up. It's not safe."

"I know. I just keep thinking about the dealerships we're already scheduled to be at and also again about how much it's going to cost to stay here for three or four days. We can't stay outside in this weather."

"Exactly, you can't. You especially can't keep driving in it. I can call the dealerships and let them know why you'll be late and you can make up the time later. It's not worth risking yours and Scooter's life over." I agreed with him, but I was frustrated as hell. When I hung up the guys at the dealership re-iterated what my dad said. There was a guy working there named Dan. He was this

SCOOTINAMERICA-INSIDE MY HELMET

super-tall middle-aged guy with long white hair. If you close your eyes and picture an older hard-core biker…that would be Dan.

"You can stay with me if you need a place. I don't have anything fancy, but I can offer you a room and a warm bed for a few days."

I knew everyone was right and since he was kind enough to offer us a place to stay I didn't have much argument left. "That sounds great, thank you."

When the dealership closed for the day I followed Dan home. He once again apologized for it "not being much," as he showed us around. It may have been a palace for all I was concerned about the size of it. It was warm and I appreciated the hell out of his willingness to open up his home to us. He showed us our room and then told me to "help myself" to whatever I needed. It was getting close to dinner time so I made my way into the kitchen and opened up the refrigerator. It was empty. It wasn't empty as in the way some guy's refrigerators are empty, with beer and condiments…It was completely and utterly empty. It was like if you walked into Sears and went to the appliance department and opened a refrigerator…empty. Dan walked up behind me as I looked inside and said,

"I told you I didn't have much." I laughed and wondered what this guy ate. That was when he reached over and opened up the freezer, it was literally full from top to bottom with ribeye steaks. There were like seventy of them.

"Wow." He took the word "carnivore" to a whole new level.

He laughed. "The meat guy comes by the dealership once a month and hooks me up. He gives me a really good deal." He took a can of beans out of the cabinet and we fried the steak without a stitch of any kind of condiment on it and we ate it for dinner with the beans.

SCOOTINAMERICA-INSIDE MY HELMET

While we ate he told me a little about his background.

"I belong to an MC club called the "Chula Chasers.""

Laughing I said, "That's some name."

"Yeah, it all started back in the early '90's when a group of friends took a road trip to Oklahoma. They stopped to fill up at this little station and there was this kid there. He looked them over and said,

"Are y'all a gang?"

"One of the guys laughed and said, "Nope, we're Chula Chasers from Fort Worth, Texas," and that's how the group was born. We ordered t-shirts and sold them and it was decided that we would donate the profits from that to MH/MR of Tarrant County. That's a place that supports the mentally ill and developmentally disabled people of the county and their families. From there we started participating in toy runs and wounded soldier rides and this past year we raised over fifty-six thousand dollars for our cause."

"Wow, that's incredible." I felt honored to have met this guy and I had nothing but respect for what he and his club were doing, and the more I talked to him, the more interesting I found him to be. He even introduced me to one of the founding members of the "Warlocks." This was a club I had heard of. It came out of a dream that thirteen sailors came up with back in 1967 when they were on an eight month deployment with the Sixth Fleet. They were aboard the Aircraft Carrier U.S.S. Shangri-La in the middle of the Mediterranean Sea and thinking about what they wanted to do when their service was over. They decided to form a motorcycle club. They agreed on the name Warlocks and one of them designed the Blazing style Eagle which to this day is still on the backs of all their vests. Not all thirteen followed through with the idea once they actually went home, but at least one of them did. The first chapter was founded in Orlando Florida that year and the Mother club still exists. They now host several chapters in the U.S., England and Germany. They have nomads scattered throughout

SCOOTINAMERICA-INSIDE MY HELMET

the states and abroad. As I listened to Dan's stories I thought again how much I loved this part of what I was doing and reminded me how fortunate I was to be here.

The second night that I was there Dan said,

"Hey I'm going out to spend some time with my girl tonight, but if you're feeling stir crazy there's a pretty cool club not far from here I like to go. It's called The Electric Cowboy. It's a good place for you to pick up a little of the local flavor."

With all this bad weather I was definitely beginning to feel stir crazy. Plus, some of the best little bars I'd found on the trip so far came about through recommendations of the locals. I got there and as the name would imply, it was all cowboy. I love country music, but I'm not really a western dance kind of guy. Nonetheless, I was fascinated by this place, the décor was great...all western, and I got a big kick out of watching the people on the dance floor dance the two-step in circles...I was also impressed with the way these Texas men treated their ladies. As a matter of fact it seemed to be practically illegal to not treat them well. That first night I was just interested in getting out of the house and striking up a conversation with some of the locals. I sat down at the bar next to this young couple. The guy was kind of a young hip-hop looking dude with a really cute little girlfriend. He started out asking me about Scooter which is probably how ninety percent of my conversations with strangers on the road begin, and from there I told him about the trip and what we were doing. He was going on and on about how cool that was and how cool I was and suddenly he said,

"Man, you should just take my girlfriend right now," and he kind of play-pushed her towards me. I thought that was a little odd, but right at that exact moment Sam Elliot's twin walked by. I kid you not, this guy was like the last of the original cowboys and when he heard what the young man said he stopped dead in his tracks and as soon as he did the kid kind of laughed nervously and looked up at him and said, "You walked in at the wrong time."

59

SCOOTINAMERICA-INSIDE MY HELMET

With a stone cold face and in a deep, Marlboro man voice the cowboy said, "Damn sure did." Then he just went on about his business. It was great.

Watching the action on the dance floor really made me wish that I could dance like that. It also made me nostalgic for the days when I had a lady on my arm and once again my thoughts went to Laura. It was easy to think about her at times like this because we always did have a lot of fun together. She wasn't shy about trying new things and neither was I. But now I was getting used to the idea of trying them on my own. Before the night was over I got to talking to this young guy who was giving dance lessons. This guy was high energy and fast talking and just all kinds of fun. It seemed like he really loved what he did and he was one of those people who were so enthusiastic that you could almost breathe it in when you're in the same space.

"How long are you in town?" he asked.

"I'm not sure; I'm just trying to weather this storm."

"Well it looks like the storm is going to hang in for another day or two at least. You should stop by tomorrow and take a lesson with me."

I laughed. "I don't know about that."

"Aw come on, I'm a great teacher. I'll have you swinging the ladies around the floor like a pro in one or two lessons at the most."

That didn't sound like a bad idea…and what did I really have to lose? "You know what? I might just take you up on that." By the time I left that night I'd agreed to come back the next night and take a lesson. I went to the Boot Barn in town the next day and talked the guy there into a good deal on a pair of cowboy boots. I went back for my lessons for the next two nights and by my last night in town I had pretty decently grasped the swing and the two-

SCOOTINAMERICA-INSIDE MY HELMET

step and I'd built up enough confidence in my dance skills to ask a pretty girl to dance.

It felt great to kind of relax and be able to romance a lady again. We moved seamlessly together…although it may have had to do more with the fact this this little lady had also been a competition dancer than the few steps I had learned in a short period of time. It's just another one of those things coming out of this trip that I'll get to say for the rest of my life, "Yea…I learned to two-step in Texas."

Four days and a lot of rib-eye steaks and beans later, coupled with the memories of dancing like a cowboy, the storm cleared up enough for us to head out of Fort Worth. I'd started out the week frustrated and worried about getting even more behind…and ended up grateful I'd gotten to stay. It's funny how life works that way.

Dan was more than a gracious host and a man I will call my friend for life

CHAPTER TEN

"Never let the future disturb you. You will meet it, if you have to, with the same weapons of reason which today arm you against the present."—Marcus Aurelius, Meditations.

By mid-January I had been away from home for two months and a full month of it had been spent driving the long, straight roads of Texas. Often times I would start out in the morning with that serene feeling I get from the simple freedom of getting on my bike and out on the open road. Most of the time that feeling would last through the day...but it wasn't unheard of to have a day where my emotions took me on a rollercoaster ride and I had to re-think what I was doing out here.

There is so much I love about this trip and so much that I am grateful for. I love the sense of pride and accomplishment it gives me. I love that while I'm doing something worthwhile I get to sometimes just revel in the sights and sounds of this incredibly beautiful country we live in. I love meeting so many new people with such diverse backgrounds and history and making new friends and memories that I know I will carry with me for a lifetime. But somedays instead of concentrating on all of those things that I love, I was forced to think about all of the things that try to get in the way of that, and where the rollercoaster ride commences.

For starters, social media is my friend...and my enemy. My followers are multiplying daily and as great as that is and as much as this cause I am riding for benefits from that, it's work that needs to be tended to daily. I believe that I owe something to all of these generous and kind-hearted people who check in on me and Scooter every day and wish us well and get the word out about what we're doing. I feel like I have to at least say hello to the people who share my pictures and videos and do my best to respond to their questions. Unfortunately that was usually easier said than done.

SCOOTIN AMERICA-INSIDE MY HELMET

I spent my days riding the highways and the backroads and the mountain paths…and in between I stopped at the dealerships. I participated in the local events and along the way and I took care of Scooter and I plotted out our meals and lodging every day. Sometimes when fatigue pulled at me so heavily that my muscles and extremities felt like steel weights, I had to forego the sleep in order to take care of the business. Other times when I was at a dealership doing meet and greets I would slip into the bathroom and send up a post. I've done a lot of my posts from a bathroom in the back of many Harley Davidson dealerships. The reality is that "down time" out here on the road, doesn't really exist. I have literally dedicated this year of my life to what we're doing. I initially looked at the trip from mostly a "fun and adventurous angle…but the longer I was out here, the more important reaching higher goals for these kids became. It was my job at this point and like everything else I'd ever done, I wanted desperately for it to be a success. I honestly didn't regret giving up my downtime, but it would take a lot of getting used to and figuring out.

A lot of other things weighed on my mind as I rode along hypnotized by the scenery and the asphalt and the music in my ears. When I began this journey one of my big hopes was that Harley-Davidson would eventually be willing to have their corporate office work with me on this mission. A large percentage of the dealerships that my father has contacted about our mission have been excited about it and welcomed us with open arms. But as individual as people are, so are the dealerships. They're independently owned and operated and that means we run into a lot of different personalities. Along the way there have been those that Dad has contacted who don't really have an interest in helping us out. Everyone has their own story and who knows what theirs is…I do my best not to judge, but that doesn't make it any less disheartening when my father is not treated well, or Scooter and I show up and we're told that the marketing director didn't tell any employees or customers that we were coming. My dad is diligent about what he does and I know that he's spoken to someone at each one of the dealerships. How that information is passed along varies from one dealership to the next so who's to say the message just didn't get delivered to the right person? Nevertheless it made it

SCOOTINAMERICA-INSIDE MY HELMET

really difficult if Scooter and I showed up to a dealership that had no idea we were coming. Sometimes we were blown away by the amount of donations…and sometimes we left with nothing at all. All of that left my analytical, marketing brain scrambling to come up with more and better ways for us to do things.

I have had the thought more than once that if Harley-Davidson's corporate office were on board with our cause that would be a significant help when it came to reaching out to the independent dealers. The problem with that is Harley Davidson already works closely with one major charity and ours isn't it. When I made contact with them about the American Legion Scholarship Fund, they weren't interested in sponsoring us at all. In their defense, they did ask me why I didn't do what I was doing for The Wounded Warrior Project instead. It was the charity they already sponsored. I had made my choice by that time however and I wasn't willing to abandon these kids. I picked this cause for more than one reason, but the children who would benefit from it have always been foremost in my mind.

Unfortunately, dealing with an organization the size of the American Legion has not always been easy either. Some of the angst in my head came directly from my struggles with getting them to recognize what we were doing. My local chapter has been nothing but stellar in their efforts to help and their appreciation of what we're doing. But, along the road before we stop at a dealership either my dad or I will send an email to the local chapter of the American Legion and request they send a representative to join me. Out of the first three hundred or so dealerships I visited, I've had maybe twenty of them show up. I do know that a lot of these posts are manned by older and even elderly vets. A lot of these guys don't have a clue about social media or how to use it so that's one of the roadblocks. In the hopes of generating more interest, I visited the huge, downtown offices of the American Legion once in Indianapolis. I was given a cursory meeting with a few guys that seemed slightly bored with the whole affair…and I left confused and unsatisfied.

SCOOTINAMERICA-INSIDE MY HELMET

The absolute truth is that as much as I love what I'm doing there are days…when the gloom begins to suffocate me I'm like a kid away from their friends and family at summer camp…I just want to go home. I want to eat a real meal and sleep in a real bed. I want to sit on a comfortable couch and watch television. I want to take a pretty girl out on a date on Saturday night. The funny thing is, that every time all of these thoughts begin to unravel inside of my head and I feel like I want to give up…something happens to remind me exactly what and who I am doing this for.

I remember sitting on a couch at a dealership one day after the meet and greet was completed. A middle-aged lady came up and stood beside me. I could feel her energy and just knew she had something to say. When I looked at her closely I could see sadness in her eyes as she said,

"Could I take a picture with you and Scooter on my bike?"

"Yeah, of course," I gave her a smile. She smiled back, but it didn't reach her eyes.

We went outside and posed for the picture and then she said, "I just wanted to tell you how great I think what you're doing out here is." Then, she broke down in tears. I could tell they were tears that she'd been trying to hold back, but once she lost control of them it was heart-breaking. I led her over to a place where we could sit and she wiped her eyes and said,

"My son came home not too long ago from…over there. I was so happy to have him back. My biggest fear had always been that he would come home in a box. It didn't take me long to realize that I really didn't have the boy I sent over there back and I never will…but I was still feeling lucky because I knew so many mothers never got theirs back at all. My poor boy had PTSD…he saw so many terrible things and I'm sure he didn't even tell me about the bulk of them. One thing he did tell me and I could just see how it was tearing him apart as he did, was that he was in a Humvee and was forced to run over a child…" she paused and I could see it was getting harder for her to fight back the tears again. I felt so

SCOOTINAMERICA-INSIDE MY HELMET

helpless…how do you comfort a mother that's in so much obvious pain? I hoped that just listening would help, so I waited silently and when she was ready she went on, "See they are fighting a different kind of enemy over there. They use children and women as weapons. We here in America find these things unspeakable and it's almost unbearable for us to cope with." She lost her battle with the tears then and they rolled freely down her face as she said, "He ended up taking his own life. He just couldn't deal with all of that ugly in his head. He came home, but I lost him anyways." I let her cry and as I witnessed her unfathomable grief I tried to imagine what her son must have gone through over there. I wondered how many times he felt like crying because he just wanted to be at home. How many nights did he wish for a real bed or the simplicity of watching his favorite program on TV? So many things we take for granted here that these young men and women willing give up…so that we can continue to enjoy them. I sat with this lady who herself had made the ultimate sacrifice for our country. She'd given her son just as the children I was riding for had given their fathers or mothers. While we sat there, she waffled between smiles and tears as she told me more about her boy. When she was ready to leave she gave me a warm hug and said, "I just wanted to thank you for what you're doing. I can't tell you how much it means."

"You can't imagine what it means to me to hear the mother of one of our brave soldiers tell me that," I told her honestly. The reality that I was doing something good here was once again setting in. Day in and out I ride this emotional rollercoaster…but when I get a hug from a grieving mother, or hear one say she's waiting for hers to come home…or listen to a widow whose husband didn't make it or hear about a child that will never meet his father…or I get to experience the absolute awe of an aging veteran who shakes to his feet in order to salute me…any gloom I'm feeling dissipates just like that. At the end of each day I don't dwell on a dealership I had a hard time with or the things I sold in order to be here. I'm even learning how to cope with my loneliness by substituting the true happiness that helping others brings me. I've quickly learned that no amount of money…either the money I gave up to be here or any money a sponsor might give me, would be a substitute for the peace I feel in my heart each day

SCOOTINAMERICA-INSIDE MY HELMET

now. I was terrified to let go of everything that I'd worked for and face the world stripped and alone…but I know now that my fears were unfounded. All I feel now is content and free.

Me and Scooter entering California

CHAPTER ELEVEN

"There is science, logic, reason; there is thought verified by experience. And then there is California."—Edward Abbey

It was the middle of January and the traffic in Southern California was no joke. We were heading towards Orange County HD and as we did, the cars inched along and stretched out in a seemingly infinite line in front of us. I had to be alert as people got frustrated and tried to cut in and out of spaces their cars could hardly fit into. The squeal of tires as someone hit their brakes or the scream of a horn when someone else's patience ran out penetrated the sounds of my bike and even the helmet that I wore. Occasionally the wail of a siren would add to the noise and I'd marvel at the patience it must take to drive an emergency vehicle in this mess. While I carefully maneuvered the bike in and out of the maze I realized that to most of these people this was just another day in the city. They commuted to or from their jobs or ran their errands in this every day. It was one part of the rat-race that I'd gladly taken a break from. I'd also woken up that morning to another text from Laura. This one said,

"Adam…If I put "him" on a plane and send him home, will you take me back?"

I'd thought long and hard about it way before I got that text. I still loved Laura. I cared a great deal about her happiness. Sometimes I'd even text her just to make sure she was okay. I remember hearing she was in the hospital once and reaching out to her to see if she needed anything…but that came from a place of caring about her and what happened to her.

When I got texts like this from her it was like scraping the scab off the wound and watching it bleed out all over again. This particular day I did what I had done countless times before…I reached out to a good friend of mine. I called my friend Trey and I told him what her message said. His response was,

SCOOTINAMERICA-INSIDE MY HELMET

"So she's living with this guy…but she's willing to break up with him…if you'll take her back?"

"That's what she says."

"But if you don't take her back, she stays with him?"

"Yep…I guess."

"So you tell me how you feel about that."

"You know how I feel about it. It's screwed up. It's like her reality is twisted that she's calling me while she's still got this guy in her bed. Those aren't my morals and she should know that."

"Right, she should, but once again she's thinking about Laura and what Laura wants. Laura doesn't want to be alone." I think when you've been cheated on; you're always kind of looking for a way to assuage your wounded heart. I had to wonder when I really thought about that, if maybe that was why she had cheated. Was it simple desperation because she hated being alone so badly and I was traveling so much? It helped my ego and confidence to believe that. I could at least feel that if that was the case, it wasn't something that I'd done…or that I wasn't good enough. Trey went on to say, "Listen Adam, she's watching your trip on social media and she sees you living the life. She's envious and she sees what she missed out on. You're going to have to just cut her off man…or she's going to keep holding you back."

"You're right…I know you're right. Sometimes I guess I just need to hear someone else say it out loud."

"Any time, buddy." I thought over that conversation as I weaved in and out of the traffic. Trey is right and I have to stay focused on what's in front of me and not behind.

****

SCOOTINAMERICA-INSIDE MY HELMET

We finally made it to Orange County Harley Davidson. This dealership began advertising for us at least two weeks before we arrived and that day they opened up their dealership to us and the community with a free barbecue. When we arrived they had someone singing the National Anthem and a giant flag flew high on the flagpole. The place was packed and during the event a bunch of little kids ran around with buckets and jars collecting donations. When all was said and done they had collected $2800.00 for our cause. I was practically brought to tears by their generosity as well as the way they welcomed us with open arms, and the next day we were joined by a small army of bikes that escorted us from there to our next stop. People like this chase away the clouds of discouragement that have occasionally intruded on my thoughts during this journey. It is people like this that make up the very fabric of America and regardless of what you read in the news and see on social media every day, these are still the true backbones of our great country. There are still more people who care than there are those who don't and once again I had to be thankful for this journey helping me discover that.

Mine and Scooter's adventures with the coyotes that night on the side of a mountain started just about fifty miles up the California coast from that dealer in Orange. We visited a place called Bartels Harley Davidson in Santa Monica and I met some really cool people. There was a couple I met there that had friends who worked with a production company.

"Hey we're going to this party tonight. Why don't you come with us and you can meet some of them? Maybe we can even get you hooked up with a place to stay."

I was already worn thin from being up so early, but even so, I didn't want to pass up on this possible opportunity. I still had hopes that we might be able to score some kind of reality show and officially get the word out about what we were doing. Publicity increases participation and that increases donations. Besides being able to respect the man I have become, getting those donations was tantamount to this ride being a success. I decided I could push myself a few hours more and said,

SCOOTINAMERICA-INSIDE MY HELMET

"That sounds great, thanks."

We went to a local club and I met some more really fun people before we all headed back to this house party in the hills at about one a.m. By this time I was beyond exhausted and I still hadn't met anyone from a production company...but, I was still holding out hope. Hope was a big part of this new lifestyle of mine. Without it, there would be days that I would never be able to push through to the next.

As the morning began to wear on though, the fatigue began to press in on me. By two a.m. I was just done. I'd been up going non-stop for something like sixteen hours at that point. It didn't seem like we were going to be offered that warm shelter they had mentioned earlier in the day and I wasn't going to impose upon them by asking. Instead, I said good-bye and thanked them and Scooter and I saddled up on the warhorse and headed up into what will forevermore be termed in my head as, "Coyote country."

That night after I had finally run them off and I lay there listening to the sounds of them in the distance was when I began questioning what I was doing. It wasn't going to be the last time on this trip that I would ask myself that either. If it wasn't for that hope I refused to let go of, or the fact that those discouraging thoughts were always soon overridden by something good happening, I may have given up. The fact was that the pros of this entire trip heavily outweighed the cons. Luckily the last fight with the coyotes drove them away for the rest of the night and I was able to get at least a little bit of rest. I slept on edge, waking up at the sound of every rustle...but the yips and calls of the predators were at least far off in the distance now. We had jumped another hurdle and each time that happened it gave me a little more strength to go on.

The next morning I woke up to a bright and beautiful California winter day. Curious still about the coyotes, I walked over to where I had last seen them the night before. I looked down over the edge of the mountain and realized we were sitting on top of a breathtakingly gorgeous view. Down below us was a valley and

SCOOTINAMERICA-INSIDE MY HELMET

nestled into it was this huge old dried up dam surrounded by acres of natural beauty. It was one of those sights that although your eyes are seeing it, your brain hardly believes it. It was surreal and I had to go down there and see it up close. Scooter and I hiked down and as I walked around and looked at this historical sight, I realized that I would have probably never seen it, if not for this trip and the unplanned events that went along with it. It was dawning on me that sometimes the unexpected things turn out to inspire more than those that I had planned.

I sat down in the valley for a bit and breathed in the fresh, warm air and basked in the sunny California morning. Scooter and I eventually hiked all the way down to the Dam and I pulled out my pocket stove right there and cooked myself a cup of hot coffee. I sat there on top of the dam and as I drank my Joe and reveled in the beauty of it all it hit me what a contrast this was from last night and the feelings that were weighing me down. That morning I felt completely relaxed and at peace. I sat there for hours feeling like the luckiest man alive and once again the positive feelings I had completely obliterated the negative ones that I'd had the night before. Without a doubt, I was ready to keep going.

This place although I didn't know it then, had already survived eight decades. Since dried up by a drought in the '60's it's been used during the filming of over a hundred Hollywood films. It's one of those hidden but iconic treasures that America has to offer, one of many that had such a profound effect on me that it will stay a part of me long after this trip has ended and I've moved on with my life. As ironic as it seems, it was a sight that if not for the coyotes, I probably would have never seen.

Despite any setbacks or second-guessing, I had a fantastic time in Southern California and while Scooter and I were there, we collected a large amount of donations for the kids. I was sad to leave it behind, but there was so much more fun to come in the Golden State. I was actually able to cross off more than one thing off my bucket list while I was there and the first one came about the time we hit Hollister.

SCOOTINAMERICA-INSIDE MY HELMET

I'd had another long day and it was already around eight p.m. and I still hadn't found a place to rest our heads for the night. One of the best ways I've found to meet people in the local communities is to stop in at the local bars or restaurants they might hang out in. I've found that people often tend to let their guard down and are willing to make conversation with a stranger in a place where they feel safe and comfortable. I searched the internet looking for what might look like a "biker bar" and found a local spot. Once we arrived we sat down next to a middle-aged man and his wife. They asked me about Scooter and somewhere during the conversation about my travels the talk turned to our bucket lists. As we took turns naming off our lists I said,

"Going up in a glider," as one of mine.

The man literally lit up. "You're kidding, right?"

"Absolutely not, one of these days I plan on doing it." At first I thought he was questioning the sanity of the adventure until he said,

"How about tomorrow?"

"What?"

He laughed. "Guess what I do for a living?"

"I'll go out on a limb here and say something with gliders?"

"You got it. As a matter of fact, I own a local glider company."

"Now I have to ask you if you're kidding."

He laughed again. "Nope, I'm dead serious. I'd be honored to take you up."

SCOOTINAMERICA-INSIDE MY HELMET

"Oh my God…I'm in shock." I really was. How does that just happen? "I would love that…but unfortunately I have to take off really early. I'm scheduled to be at my next stop at six a.m." Although hitting my bucket list is always a big personal part of the trip my schedule comes first.

He shrugged. "I got nothing against early. We can take her up and watch the sun rise."

"Really?" I felt like a kid on Christmas morning. I almost pinched myself, that's how hard it was to believe. I was outrageously excited and when I left there and found us a little spot to sleep, I could barely close my eyes. I couldn't wait.

I showed up the next morning right on time and I have to admit, just a bit nervous. The thought of going up without any power was a little frightening…but not so much that it hindered my excitement. We went up and as the sun rose we were gliding over the mountains and then the ocean. Being in a glider is so different from being in an airplane. I spent countless hours and days flying around the world as part of that corporate life I left behind. In an airplane you have the sounds of the engine and sometimes the propellers…but one of the most incredible things about being up in a glider is the serene quiet. All you hear is the wind flowing across the fuselage and the razor thin wings and it's more like natural music than noise. We floated across Monterey Bay, the San Andreas Fault and the first Spanish mission in California as well as thousands of acres of beautiful land and water. The landing was as smooth as soaring across the skyline, and as soon as we were on the ground I said,

"That was incredible. I have to do that again someday." If I had time, I would have wanted to do it again right then.

"I'm glad you enjoyed yourself. I have to tell you that today was a first for me to."

"In what way?"

SCOOTINAMERICA-INSIDE MY HELMET

"Well, I have been doing this for over thirty years and this is the first time a dog has gone up."

I laughed, "Well, Scooter isn't your average dog. He's always been a bit of the adventurous type." My brave little dog is experiencing a once in a lifetime adventure right beside me every day and I don't think he misses that 62 inch TV any more than I do...which is not at all.

**My morning view of that dried up dam. It was a hike
down but well worth it**

CHAPTER TWELVE

"If I weren't doing what I'm doing today... I'd be traveling around the world on the back of a motorcycle."—Donna Karan

The fun in California continued all along the coast. The closer I got to San Francisco the more pumped and excited I got. When I was a kid one of the things I'd always wanted to see was the Golden Gate Bridge. It's one of the most iconic landmarks in the United States and as I got older I dreamt of riding my bike across it. I became emotional as I approached it, another check off the bucket list. My heart was racing and the only way I can describe the feelings I had as the War Horse, Scooter and I drove the one point seven miles from one side of the bay to the other was: exhilarating. It was an entirely sensory experience and I enjoyed it to the fullest. As my mind realized that I was finally achieving a dream that I'd had since childhood…my eyes took in the sheer beauty of the misty Bay itself. Every sight, sound and smell was amplified a thousand times and as I reached the other side I couldn't help but think that this is how life is meant to be lived. It's way too short to spend with regrets and each day on the road provides more evidence to my heart and soul that all dreams are attainable. For most of us, as we grow from childhood to adulthood we get so busy with the act of attaining the things that our neighbors have and that society tells us that we need…we tend to forget the magic and wonder of those simple dreams we had that meant so much. Riding that bridge was further proof to me that I was doing the right thing here. My soul was happy. Northern California was delivering me the adventure I had dreamt of for years, and as soon as I had achieved one it seemed like another one quickly followed. This was a lesson, a lesson I will forever carry with me. It is teaching me that the beauty of life is held within our soul, not our image.

I'd heard about the giant redwoods and as a little guy, they were almost a mythical idea…thousand year old trees that you could actually drive a car through. It doesn't get much more

SCOOTINAMERICA-INSIDE MY HELMET

remarkable than that. Today there are only three drive-thru trees
that are still open to the public. They're all located along Highway
101 at different points collectively known as "The Avenue of
Giants." These three trees are the last of a true piece of Americana
and for me, seeing them and driving through one of them was a
must. I drove through the "Chandelier Tree," in a town called
Leggett in Mendocino County and it is another one of those
memories I will hold onto forever. These are memories that I could
easily never have experienced had I continued with my life the way
it was going. Thanks to that shifting moment when I decided to let
go and take the risk and I made a decision and rode it out…I was
here today. It had been a risk, but I've quickly come to realize that
having what most people would define as "nothing," to me was
everything. These adventures were the payoff for the gamble I had
taken.

        In its broadest sense, nature is everything. It can refer to
the physical world or life in general and although we as humans are
a part of this phenomenon, we often see ourselves as completely
separate entities. As I experience one more natural thrill after the
other on this trip, it becomes easier for me to see myself as an
integral part of it. I've learned the hard way that people come and
go and I've freed myself from the binds that things often come
along with…but nature is always there. It possesses a beauty that is
constantly evolving and changing…but never ending. Nature is the
one constant we will always have and the idea of us as humans
taking care of it was becoming more important to me than ever
before.

            ****

        As we continued our trek up North, I remember looking at
this river that wound around for miles through the forest. It was
the bluest river that I'd ever seen. It literally captivated me. Along
the way north we also stopped to visit the Big Foot Museum in
Willow Creek. Whether you're a believer or not it's an interesting
little place. Willow Creek in and of itself is interesting. It's only 300
feet above sea level but the way the mountains surround it makes
you feel much higher. The weather in Northern California in the

80

SCOOTINAMERICA-INSIDE MY HELMET

winter time is fickle. One minute it would overflow with sunshine and warmth and the next, the sky would turn dark and brooding, threatening to bring down a storm. Sometimes it was just plain indecisive…it would flirt with ideas of warmth and cold, sometimes turning into a freezing fog and others a warm, wet mist. This one particular evening as we headed up towards Redding it was misting hard. I was soaking wet and so was all of my gear. I was also chilled to the bone, and exhausted. I knew if I just stopped and found a place to camp that it was very unlikely my gear would dry out before morning, so when we came up on this gorgeous little town in the valley I decided we would get a place for the night and hopefully the use of a dryer so that I wouldn't have to put on wet gear the next day.

I found a rustic group of cabins along the river that this sweet little old lady rented out. I rented one and laid my gear out in the warm room to dry. Later that night Scooter and I walked around the town and we ended up finding this cool little mountain bar. I sat there for a while talking to the locals. Again, it's one of my favorite things about this trip. Getting to know the people is as fascinating to me as exploring the places. There was a pretty young lady there and I was the new guy in town so she was paying a lot of attention to me and coming on strong. When I got ready to leave she asked me if I wanted to go to a party.

"Nah thanks though. I'm exhausted and I have to get up early." She looked disappointed and when she realized that Scooter and I were walking she said, "I can get you a ride back to your cabin." The weather was still wet and cold so I said,

"That sounds great, thanks."

Not long after she made a call, a young guy in a big jacked up pick-up drove up. She introduced us and as it turned out, he was a really nice guy. I talked with him on the ride back to the cabin about what we were doing and before they left me at the cabin the kid said,

"Hey, I've got some really good moonshine here. Do you want to try some?"

"Sure." He handed me a clear jar and I took a taste. I was surprised at how smooth this stuff was. I'd had moonshine before that tasted like paint thinner and burned all the way down. This was honestly the best I'd ever had and I told him as much. As I tried to hand it back to him he said,

"I love your story it's like one big adventure. I'm sure you meet all kinds out here on the road. Take it with you and when you meet someone really cool, share it with them."

I really liked that idea. "I'll be sure to do that, thanks." I jumped out of the truck and Scooter and I bunked down for a warm dry nights rest.

**Scooter living my childhood dream alongside of me as we
cross the Golden Gate Bridge**

CHAPTER THIRTEEN

"I'm gonna break, I'm gonna break my, I'm gonna break my rusty cage and run" — *Johnny Cash*

It was a few days later when we drove into Folsom. It was drizzling slightly but it wasn't freezing and I was always thankful for that. We made our stop at Folsom Harley Davidson and the people there were amazing. They let me take off my gear and hang it all over the place to dry. I literally had it laying out everywhere in the middle of their showroom. People were walking up to the register to buy hundreds of dollars in gear and were sidestepping my soaked snow hat and stretched out bandanas and nobody seemed to care at all. It took us hours to get everything laid out and dried up, and the locals were happy to share stories with me as we waited on my stuff to dry.

We also picked up $150.00 for the kids and while we were there, I met a really nice lady. She was a biker and a nice looking "inked-up" lady who was kind enough to offer me and Scooter a place to stay in her home. I was so grateful to not have to stay out in the rain. I accepted and when we got to her place she made us dinner and we sat and talked like we'd known each other for years. We talked about my trip and the break-up of my marriage before I left. She also told me about her life and her most recent relationship. Her ex-boyfriend was a Hells Angel and she had been having problems dating because of it. Just because of people's own silly fears and prejudices she found out that no one wanted to date an Angel's ex-old lady. She seemed to genuinely appreciate having someone to talk about it.

After dinner and our talk we were both emotional. It felt like in that short time we'd formed a tight bond. When she invited me to join her and some of her biker friends for a drink at one of the local bars, I readily accepted. Scooter was tuckered out so he stayed at home and got to rest where it was nice and warm. She

SCOOTINAMERICA-INSIDE MY HELMET

rode with me on my bike and since I'd told her earlier how badly I wanted to see Folsom prison we stopped to see it along the way. It was really a cool place to look at all lit up in the dark. It's an old prison, the second oldest in California and the one that Johnny Cash made famous when he sang about it.

We got to this bar and her friends from the dealership were there. These were all hard-core riders and a fun group of people. I had eaten earlier and while we were there I had two drinks over the course of several hours, while telling stories of the road and learning about the local flavor...I'm a big guy so I know without a doubt that two drinks is nowhere near enough to put me over the legal limit or even give me enough of a buzz that I needed to worry about driving legally or safely. I don't get on the bike when I'm drunk...ever.

So after a while we all decided to call it a night. We were laughing and having a good time and we took the fun with us to the parking lot. After saying good-night to everyone we saddled up and rode off into the night. We all hit the road together and started out from down town. The ride took us to a big hill like you often find in that part of Cali. As we did, these guys decided to "get on it". Of course I was right there enjoying the thrill of the Warhorse beside them. There is just something about the sound of a group of bikes riding off that says freedom, although this time it looked as how it could be just the opposite. Almost instantaneously red and blue lights lit up the street behind us. We pulled over and the first question the cops asked was if I had been drinking.

"Yeah, I've had two drinks over the last two or three hours," I told them.

"Why are your eyes so red?"

"I'm just tired." That was absolutely true. I'm always tired.

"Well we're going to have to administer a field sobriety test."

SCOOTINAMERICA-INSIDE MY HELMET

I sat there and answered a long list of questions about who I was and what I was doing prior to them stopping me and then they had me do the normal "walk the line" and "recite the alphabet" thing. I told them my story as well in hopes of explaining just why I was so tired that my eyes were shot through with red lines. In the middle of this two other cops pulled up and were standing by as well. When I finished, thinking that was going to be it, one of the cops said,

"The results of the test force me by law to ask you to take a breathalyzer test." Before I could say anything he went on to say, "Now, you can refuse it...it's up to your own discretion. If you do refuse, its then up to our discretion whether or not we think you're drunk enough to haul you down town." Something about the way he said it seemed to me as if he was telling me to refuse so they could let me go on my way. I knew that I would pass if I took it...but again, I thought they were just trying to give me friendly advice.

"Okay then, I'll refuse it. I trust your judgment that I'm not drunk." I said. The officers went back and talked for a bit before the cop that offered it in the first place said,

"I'm going to have to take you in..."

"What? You just told me that I could refuse it."

"You can and I did. I also said that then it's up to my discretion...and I'm still saying your eyes don't look good. Turn around and put your hands behind your back." I was suddenly freaking out inside. I knew as soon as I got to the jail and took the test they would have to let me go...but in the meantime if word of this got out, what would it do to my cause.

"What about my bike?"

"It'll be impounded." My head was going crazy now calculating how much that was going to cost. Shit! I looked at the lady I was with and said,

SCOOTINAMERICA-INSIDE MY HELMET

"Will you look after Scooter? This shouldn't take too long…" I hoped.

"Of course," she said.

The officer led me to the car and as he was putting me in the back seat I said, "Can I just take the breathalyzer test?"

"Nope you had your chance" he said

Once again before I could speak another word…which at that point was probably good…the other officer said, "Just let him take the breathalyzer."

They discussed it amongst themselves again as I sat there and waited. The ramifications of this ran rampant through my mind. My active imagination had my arrest splashed all over social media. I could almost see the disappointment in the eyes of those that believed in me. I wasn't drunk, but after the fact how was I going to convince anyone of that? By the time they finally came back and told me they decided to let me blow in the tube, I'd worked myself up from annoyance to full-blown anxiety. I was too anxious to even feel relieved at that point. They had me blow into that damn machine three times as everyone stood around wondering what the results would be. It was all for nothing because as I knew I would, I blew way under the legal limit. They had to let me go, but my nerve endings were still on fire. I quelled the anxiety as I drove away by telling myself to just file it away as another adventure on the road. A smile crossed my face as it suddenly dawned on me…I "walked the line" in Folsom. Ole Johnny Cash would be proud.

When we got back to her place I remembered the moonshine and what the kid had told me. She was the first person I shared it with as we sat up and talked into the night. I felt like I wanted to celebrate making a new friend as well as dodging a bullet. After that night I was careful not to drink at all if I was going to be going anywhere on the bike. Even though I know I wasn't impaired…it just wouldn't have been worth it if they'd

SCOOTINAMERICA-INSIDE MY HELMET

decided to take me in. It would have cost me a lot of money to get the Warhorse out of impound...and maybe the respect of some of my followers.

The Warhorse in the Folsom showroom prior to unloading in effort of drying out

CHAPTER FOURTEEN

"The mountains are calling and I must go."—John Muir

We headed up towards Sacramento when we left Folsom, hitting another eight dealerships in between. In Sacramento at Eagle HD we were able to collect over five hundred dollars and then from there we traveled up this amazing scenic highway that stretches out over a hundred miles through Mono and Tuolumne counties. There aren't a lot of amenities along the way…a lot of it is just pure scenery and I loved it.

After leaving there, Scooter and I finished our trek up to Jamestown. It's a really cool little historic town up near the top of Tuolumne County. It was an old mining town during the California gold rush now it's listed as a California historical landmark. It's also been used in the filming of many Hollywood movies and television shows because of its historical spots and its relationship to the railroad. It's a really neat little place with a lot of cool old trains and buildings that I enjoyed exploring. While we were there, the owner of the dealership in town kindly opened up his home to Scooter and me. He was a super nice man and we were treated like royalty. He made us fish tacos for dinner and he was genuinely excited about my ride. That night I shared some of that moonshine with him like the kid had told me too. It was cool knowing that it was only for people like this that I'd formed some kind of instantaneous bond with. It was also amazing to think about how often that happened on this trip.

The next morning, this man and some of his friends from the dealership saddled up some of the bikes right off the showroom floor and escorted us out of Jamestown and all the way to Yosemite. With our entourage we made our way up New Priest Grade which is a road that gains about 1000 feet in altitude in just a few miles. It's so pretty up there that there are almost no words to describe it. Once again it felt surreal…like my brain could barely process it. I was beginning to adjust to the overstimulation of my senses that came along with this ride and I loved every minute of it.

SCOOTINAMERICA-INSIDE MY HELMET

We passed Big Oak Flat and Groveland two other quaint little small towns and we continued west past the Rim of the World which is a scenic look-out across a gorgeous vista along Highway 120 on the way to Yosemite. From there we drove up another forty miles with each mile seemingly bringing us closer to the mountains that I could see rising on the horizon. Some of them looked like sheer rock rising up out of the trees and reaching for the sky and others were like giant piles of dirt covered with soft pine blankets. There were trees on either side of us and they rose up so high that in places they completely blocked out the sun. Eventually we came to the Big Oak Flat entrance to the park and that's where the rest of our new friends from Jamestown left us.

I was spellbound as we drove through the park. The mountains and rock formations rose up around us. There was Half Dome and Sentinel Rock and El Capitan...and all of the others that I've seen in pictures and on television. There is no way to do justice to them with words just as seeing them in a photograph or a video didn't give them that ethereal kind of appeal that they had in real life. I was honestly astounded by their beauty. I have a little mirror on my left handlebar I use to watch Scooter as we ride. I call it the Scooter Cam. With the way he looked out over the mountains and sniffed the air with his nose lifted high I could tell he too was taken back with the beauty we were riding through.

Once we were near the campgrounds, I stopped at the ranger post and told the lady there that I needed a campsite during the night. She gave me a map and told me where to look for available spots. I paid the entry fee and then I asked her,

"Can I plug in my phone?" It was completely dead and my only link to my friends, family and followers on social media.

"Um...we're really not supposed to do that," she said, "Since 9/11 we have to be so careful with electronics. I'm sorry but it's just the rules"

"I wouldn't ask, but we're doing this ride for charity..." I told her what we were doing. I explained about keeping in touch on social media and how that had become our major source of advertisement since we didn't have a budget for anything else.

She looked at the time and said, "Okay, but you have to be back to get it before six. I will be closing then and that phone will be locked up for the night"

I thanked her and promised that I would be back. After the phone was plugged in we rode into the park towards the campsites. We found a small one but before I started unloading the bike I was approached by this old man. He was probably sixty-five or seventy years old, kind of a rough looking guy who walked with ski poles. He used them like a walker or a cane. He introduced himself and said,

"I noticed you setting up, and I thought to myself anyone with a bike loaded down like that with firewood stacked atop was a true traveler. My boys and I have this campsite a little ways up the road. It's a lot nicer than this one and the fire's already set up. We're taking off if you want that one."

"Great, thank you." I followed him over to the site and he was right…it was a lot bigger and nicer. There was a picnic table and a fire pit and it was under a canopy of gorgeous old trees. I thanked him again and he and his "boys" were loading up and pulled out as I unloaded my stuff. I pitched my tent and then Scooter and I went back up to the ranger stand to get my phone and when we got back, there sat this old guy in a chair next to the fire.

"Hey," he said as he handed me a beer.

"Hey, thanks."

"I thought I'd hang out for a couple hours if you don't mind. I started out and there was a damned long line of cars. I just didn't have any desire to sit in that traffic for hours."

SCOOTINAMERICA-INSIDE MY HELMET

"Okay, sure." What was I going to say? Besides, so far some of the most interesting people I'd met on this ride had been the older Americans. This guy would turn out to be one of them. He told me that he's spent a big part of his life in the park since he was about sixteen years old, and as we talked I found out that he was probably more knowledgeable than if I'd hired a tour guide. If you asked me later on I would swear to you that this man knew every story about every major thing that ever happened in the park going back to the first Native Americans that settled there 3000 years ago, through the Mariposa war between the Natives and the white settlers. He knew a lot about the gold rush days and he told me stories about people that had come through there and made an impact on it like Chief Tenaya who fought for the Natives against the American soldiers and John Muir who spent years exploring and writing about all of the amazing landmarks inside of the park. He even knew the story of how it became a National Park. He talked about the trails by name and the mountains and rocks that he'd climbed back in his day. I was completely enamored with this old guy and I couldn't believe my luck that I just happened to stumble up on a fellow traveler who knew so much about the area and was so willing to share it.

He took me on a few of the hikes just before the sun was ready to set. After we got back he said,

"Well, I think it's about time for me to head out."

"Man, I'd really love it if you could stay and we could get some of your stories on film in the morning."

"Eh…I'm not sure. I have work tomorrow." I can be pretty persuasive when I want to be. I told him again how amazed I was at how much knowledge he had and how grateful I was that he was willing to share it with me. I guess I buttered him up some, but I meant every word of it. In the end, this super cool guy called in to work the next day so he could stay and help me share his stories with the world. That night we sat around the campfire and told stories about our life the way any two old boys might do. Before

SCOOTINAMERICA-INSIDE MY HELMET

we turned in I took out the hooch the kid had given me. There was only about an inch left in it and I told him,

"The guy who gave this to me told me to share it with cool people. I'd like you to help me finish it off." He was happy to oblige. As we drank the moonshine and sat there underneath the blanket of stars overhead, we bonded over a common love for the wide open spaces and the beauty that surrounded us. I knew that this was one of those moments in life that shouldn't be taken for granted. Some moments are meant to be remembered either for the way they made us feel or for the things they taught us. That night it was both. I felt free and happy and at peace. It was one of the moments I didn't feel alone, I didn't worry about being single I just felt privileged to be living this life. I learned a lot of things about Yosemite that I couldn't have learned from a book. I had the benefit of this man's lifetime of memories. I've always heard that people are placed in our path in life for a reason. I've never given much thought to whether or not I believe that...but I was definitely learning that some of the people I'd met on this trip that in a material sense seemed to have so little, were turning out to be some of the richest people I had ever known.

He slept on top of the picnic table that night and the next morning we went on that walk and he let me get him on video telling what he knew about the park and its landmarks. He wasn't crazy about the idea of being filmed, but he let me shoot the video anyways and he gave me a lot more great information. Before he left, he and I sat on the edge of this gorgeous cliff and looked out across the valley. Once again I wish that words would do it justice. I can honestly say that to that point it was the most beautiful place I'd ever seen.

"I have something I'd like to share with you," he said, suddenly. He reached into his shirt and pulled out a joint. I don't smoke...but this was one of those rare, "what the hell will it hurt" situations. I was out here in the middle of nowhere atop one of the largest most beautiful mountains our nation has with a guy that has truly become a friend.

SCOOTINAMERICA-INSIDE MY HELMET

"Sure, I'd love to share it with you."

**Yosemite National Park will forever hold a place within
my soul**

CHAPTER FIFTEEN

"I had to live in the desert before I could understand the full value of grass in a green ditch."—Ella Maillart, Forbidden Journey

I was sad to say good-bye to Yosemite, but looking forward still to many adventures. When we left there we rode through the center of California down to Palm Springs and ultimately straight out into the spanning void of the Mojave Desert on my way to Las Vegas. The desert possesses a brutalist kind of beauty. Everything is massive and it's lacking exterior decoration. Deep cracks run through the barren, parched soil which is baked daily by a relentless sun. The beauty is there and it's real…but if you're just passing through on your way to the concrete and glitz of Vegas, it can be easily missed. It's as if Mother Nature wanted to emphasize the massiveness of the rocks and skies here when she painted the landscape, so she sat them way off in the distance and filled the void in between with sand and rocks and Joshua trees to guard them.

Unfortunately, as beautiful as nature can be…she can also be a bitch. I came into Mojave that day into the middle of the biggest dust storm I've ever experienced. When the wind kicks into high gear across that many miles of sand and rock, the result is both blinding and painful. I endured that for about ten miles and just as I came out of that I realized I was getting low on gas. The unfettered beauty continued to stretch out before me, but the desolation also meant the amenities were few and far between…and I ran out of gas. When it happened the first time we were about thirty miles from the next gas station. The old Warhorse stopped and the only thing I could think of was to shake it…and lay it down…and try to get the residue in the tank to fuel it. I was relieved as hell when it started and I pushed on. I'd end up having to do that two more times before I came to the crest of a hill where I could see the gas station just below us. We were on the

SCOOTINAMERICA-INSIDE MY HELMET

home stretch with only about four miles to go when it happened again. That time I knew there weren't even enough fumes left, so I put it in neutral and I let it coast down that hill. I coasted all the way down and right up into the station.

With plenty of gas in the tank, we made it to Las Vegas. I've been to Vegas countless times over the years as an MMA promoter for fights and during the years that Laura and I were doing a lot of partying and heavy spending. I'd seen the inside of a lot of expensive hotels and clubs and although a lot of those memories are ones that still hold a place in my heart...this time I saw it from an entirely different perspective. Instead of looking at it from an airplane or the back of a limousine, I got my first up close and personal look at leaving Las Vegas...and I realized I'd been going about this all wrong for all of these years. Just about forty minutes outside of Vegas sits one of the most fascinating man-made marvels in our country, the Hoover Dam, and even as you look across and down into this engineering marvel, it's difficult to actually grasp the immensity of it. This dam was built during the great depression almost a hundred years ago and that in and of itself makes it a true wonder...and easy to see why it used to be considered one of the wonders of the world.

Less than twenty miles from the dam is the Valley of Fire. It's another one of those places that make you realize how small we really are and that nature is truly in charge here. I had to stop and get pictures of these huge sandstone formations that jutted up out of the ground and reached for the sky. The dark red color not only gives them their name, but a kind of surreal feeling like you're inside a painting. When you add that to the fact that you're standing in the middle of a place that was formed from the shifting of sand, uplifting and faulting and extensive erosion over the course of something like 150 million years, you once again realize just how lucky we are to be allowed to live and breathe in a place that others lived and breathed in over 3000 years ago. There are beautiful landscape areas of petrified wood and places where you can see the petroglyphs of those that came before us.

SCOOTINAMERICA-INSIDE MY HELMET

As I left Nevada and headed into Utah with my senses still reeling, I got my first glimpse of the snow-capped mountains that surrounded Zion National Park. The sandstone cliffs rise up all around you and no amount of reading about it or seeing a photograph would ever do it justice. Part of the thrill of it was that I knew we were standing next to and on top of something shaped and formed by trickles of water over millions of years. Scooter and I did some hiking and I decided that this was going to be where we would stay tonight. We camped at the highest point possible and that night I sat on the top of one of those mountains and cooked my soup over my camp stove and yet again had the privilege of gazing out at something breathtaking that I seriously doubt I would have ever seen up close and personal like this if not for this trip. Of course nothing is perfect and just to prove it I had one hell of a time trying to stake down my tarp that night. The rocks are unrelenting so I ended up just tying it to the bike and stretching it down as far as I could. It was freezing cold and my attempts at sleep that night were almost futile…but would I have given up a chance at this once in a lifetime experience because of it? Hell no. Life is all about taking the good with the bad and this trip for me is all about discovering how much more good there is in this country than I ever suspected.

****

Back when I was in Texas I'd met a young lady as I was coming through San Antonio. We were being filmed for a local news spot and the guy said,

"This is really weird; I've filmed two people doing the same thing in the same day."

"What? What do you mean, "Doing the same thing?"

"Yeah, there is this young woman who is riding her bike across country. I did an interview with her earlier today."

"Well I'll be damned. I'd love to meet her."

99

SCOOTINAMERICA-INSIDE MY HELMET

"I have her number..."

"Don't give that to me, but will you call her and give her mine? Just tell her I'd like to meet up if she'd like to and exchange stories."

He'd given her my number and she'd called me back. Her name is Danielle Lynn and I found out after I talked to her that she's going for one of the same world records that I am. She was a really cool, 30-something year old woman who had decided this was what she wanted to do...and like me, she'd made a plan and she'd set out to do it. After I left Texas we kept in touch and I was thrilled to find out she was in Arizona when I got there. She called me and I told her where we were and an hour later she met up with us on her Triumph in this place called Jerome. Jerome is an old Western town along route 66. This place is so cool. It's actually the largest existing ghost town in America. It was built originally in 1876 and destroyed by fires and rebuilt multiple times over the years. It was a booming mining town back in its day and now it stands as a piece of history. They put on gunfights in the streets and to further authenticate the fact that this was truly at one time the old west...there are wild burros that wander around literally everywhere. Scooter was a little more than freaked out by that.

Danielle camped out with us near Jerome that night and we got to know more about each other. She told me that she'd been saving up for this trip for a long time and like me, she just decided one day that it was time. She's actually like me to in the fact that she's supporting a charity along the way. She's a dress designer. She designs one dress a month for sale...so twelve in a year and then the thirteenth one she designs and strictly gives any of the proceeds to charity. As we sat and talked that first night she said,

"I wish I had planned my trip more like yours."

"What do you mean?"

SCOOTINAMERICA-INSIDE MY HELMET

"Just that it's hard for me to get any kind of support from the dealers along the way. Your trip is mapped out and they know you're coming."

I nodded and said, "To be honest, I'm a little jealous of the way you're doing things. I mean it's definitely great to have the support…but the schedule also makes it more like a job. I'm working all the time and my trip is mapped out from point A to point Z. Sometimes I get to a place and I think, "Man, I'd love to have another day…or even a week, to explore." But I have to take off because the next place is expecting me. You're able to go where you want when you want and spend as much time there as you want. I'm envious of that."

"I guess I hadn't thought of it like that."

The truth is that we were both lucky. We were both living our dream and even though occasionally I felt heavy with the weight of the responsibility I had taken on…it was nothing compared to the weight I used to carry around as every day was a struggle to make more money and have more things. I love this life…and Danielle readily admitted that she loved hers as well. We both had a lot to be thankful for and proud of.

She spent another two or three days with us and while we were together we went to Lake Havasu and saw the London Bridge. It's mind-blowing to look at this piece of history and think about it being shipped over piece by piece like a puzzle and reassembled in the desert…another one for the books. Danielle and I parted ways after that, but it was with a little bit more knowledge that we'd each gained from each other and the comfort of knowing I had another friend out there I was sure to run across again sometime in the future. We found a kindred spirit in each other and once more I was provided with a new friend I was sure I'd have for a lifetime.

**The top of that mountain was as powerful and brutal as
it was beautiful**

CHAPTER SIXTEEN

"We didn't realize we were making memories. We thought we were just having fun."--Unknown

We rode up the old Route 66 on our way to Mother Road HD in Kingman. That's an experience I would definitely recommend. It's littered with old buildings…which I love and thanks to the old ghost and mining towns all along the way it's like being thrust back in time. On the way there I had the opportunity to meet with a local H.O.G. chapter. They were having one of their monthly meetings and they invited me to sit in. I was even happier about that when I saw the agenda. This particular group wanted to talk about how to attract younger riders to their group.

There's no way for me to do a trip like this…and do it well, without learning a lot about the industry and the lifestyle. By this time I had already been to something like three hundred dealerships. I'd talked to tens of thousands of riders. I was well aware of what the brand was doing and what they were lacking. This wasn't the first time or even close to the first time that the subject of younger Harley Davidson riders had come up and it wasn't the first time I'd thought about it. I had a living document I'd created that actually listed out things that I thought they could do differently to attract the next generation. This was the first time in all of these months that anyone had asked for my insights and the first time that I'd shared them.

I sat down with these guys and two guys that happened to be riding with me at the time were invited to the table as well. This meeting lasted for about an hour and a half. Of those ninety-minutes, at least thirty of it was dedicated to talking about cataract surgery. Apparently two of the guys had the surgery recently and they all talked about how important it was to get tested for cataracts after a certain age. I was trying hard out of respect to keep a straight face, especially when the two guys with me, got up and

SCOOTINAMERICA-INSIDE MY HELMET

left. When the meeting was over and they asked me if I had any input, I had to be honest with them.

"Well, for starters if I was looking to attract a younger crowd…I might not want to dedicate a third of the meeting to talking about cataracts. I mean no disrespect by that, but it's not really a subject that a twenty, thirty or even forty-something guy is going to have a lot of interest in."

I was glad to see they'd taken it well. They laughed and joked with each other about getting "too damned old" to ride. I love meeting these old bikers, because when they're not talking about cataracts they have some great stories to tell.

We left there and moved on to the first Grand Canyon dealership, this one is in Mayer Arizona. These dealerships are owned by the same person and the staff that works at both are great people. When we walked into the first one there was a huge crowd there and they had a birthday cake for Scooter. Scooter was surprised and honored I could tell by his demeanor. It was an awesome turnout and they treated us like royalty and raised over six hundred dollars for our cause. From there we made our way to the second of the Grand Canyon dealerships, this one in Bellemont. The general manager of this one and I got to talking and he told me that he ran a little place that sold after-market bikes on the side. He was telling me about these little electric dual-sport bikes called "Zero" that he had there and before the conversation was over he said,

"Hey! How would you like to take one out for a spin?"

"Are you kidding? I'd love to." I was genuinely excited. We got on these little bikes and we rode up into the hills near Crown King up above Phoenix. It's located in the Prescott National Forest and there are anywhere between fifteen to twenty trails up in there. Some of them are straight up primitive dirt roads while others are steep and rocky and with washboards and narrow bridges. We got up there just as the sun was going down and we spent hours tearing up the trails, racing each other and having a

SCOOTINAMERICA-INSIDE MY HELMET

great time like a couple of kids and a pup. I was astounded at how fast these things could go.

When it was time for us to take a little break this guy took me to a place in the middle of nowhere in the desert called "The Yacht Club." It's a little bar where mostly locals go and it has all of these jet skis and boats around it sunken down into the sand. It's a really cool little place and we had a great time. As we got ready to leave there the sun was going down and we realized that the bike's charge was getting low so we started heading back to town. We rode down this pitch black mountain until we came to this little ghetto restaurant that was probably fifty miles from civilization. We plugged in the dirt bikes while we ate…and we didn't find out until we came back out that the outlets weren't working. His bike had about one quarter charge…and mine was completely dead.

"Now what?" I asked him. I assumed he had some experience in this area.

He thought about it for a minute before saying, "I think we can make it down on mine."

I laughed and then realized he was serious. He wanted me and Scooter to ride on that little bike with him. I was sure the two of us way exceeded the weight limit even given the fact that Scooter only weighed about six pounds. These bikes aren't built like the old Warhorse. They're made lightweight in order to maneuver the little bike trails like the ones he and I had been out playing on earlier. "I don't think that will work," I told him. "I'm pretty sure the two of us will be too heavy for that thing."

He's a pretty laid-back, easy-going kind of guy. He didn't seem upset or anxious about the situation at all. He just shrugged and said, "What choice do we have?" I looked around and had to admit that he was right. It was pitch black out here and there was no other way for us to get to the bottom of that mountain. Reluctantly, I got on the back of his bike. We went about ten miles when it became obvious that the extra weight on the bike was using even more juice and we weren't going to make it all the way down.

SCOOTINAMERICA-INSIDE MY HELMET

"You need to let me off and go on without me," I told him.

"Man we're forty miles from town. I don't want to leave you out here." We were still in the hills and I didn't want to stay out there any more than he wanted to leave me, but like he'd said earlier: What choice did we have? I insisted that he pull over and leave us and go on. It was the only way I could see any of us getting off this mountain at least before daybreak. He profusely apologized and assured me he'd be back to get me as soon as he got down the hill. "I'll text you when I'm on my way back up."

"Yeah, okay. We'll be fine. Be safe."

He took off and Scooter and I sat there in the pitch black darkness in the middle of nowhere. I looked at my phone…it was dying too. I was doing well up until that point, but I have to admit that I started to panic here just a little bit. How the hell would he find me out here if my phone dies and he can't get ahold of me? We were out here underneath a starless sky and even the moon provided very little light. I ultimately considered all of my options and decided that my best one at that point was to start walking and get as close to town as I could…at least somewhere civilized. We walked for what could have been miles…I really had no sense of time at that point. I was relieved and not surprised as we got close to a main highway at last and a police officer pulled up alongside of us.

He shined his bright light in my face and said, "Show me your hands." I put my hands up and he said, "What are you doing up here?" With a nervous laugh I told him who I was and what had happened. I had Scooter in his backpack and I let the cop see him so he didn't think I was carrying anything more lethal than a Chihuahua in there. "Well, I can't just leave you out here," he said, like music to my ears, "Come on and get in, I'll take you down further and you can call your friend and let him know."

Scooter and I gratefully climbed into the police cruiser and as he took us down the hill he let me charge my phone. By the time

SCOOTINAMERICA-INSIDE MY HELMET

he dropped us off near an exit to a main highway I had just enough
of a charge to text my new friend before the battery died again.
Scooter and I sat there for another three hours and about a
hundred different scenarios went through my mind. I knew he
wouldn't have just abandoned us, but my imagination was working
overtime and I was getting really anxious. When he did show up I
found out that his bike had run out of juice completely on the way
down too and he'd had to hitch hike back to town. It was another
fun adventure for the record books and I had another story to tell.
I was grateful to the officer as well because although sitting
alongside a major highway in the dark wasn't my idea of a good
time...I couldn't help but think of all the "fun" we may have had
on the side of that mountain in total darkness.

SCOOTINAMERICA-INSIDE MY HELMET

Logan and I were far from civilization in these Arizona Mountains

CHAPTER SEVENTEEN

**"In the end only three things matter: How much you loved.
How gently you lived, and how gracefully you let go of things
not meant for you."--Buddha**

We finished up in Arizona and headed to New Mexico.
After a stop in Santa Fe we went on to Albuquerque where we
were lucky enough to be a part of a ride for charity that turned out
about 130 riders. The ride started at Thunderbird Harley Davidson.
Thunderbird is part of Scott Fischer Enterprises and one of our
generous sponsors as was our next stop, Duke City HD. They
tuned up the Warhorse for me as well and by the time we left
Albuquerque they had helped us raise over three thousand dollars
for the kids. Their awesome generosity never seems to end. After
one more stop in New Mexico and a couple in Texas, we were in
Oklahoma. Oklahoma was an emotional roller coaster ride for me.
Part of that was Laura…again. We'd had another conversation and
during this one she had said,

*"He keeps telling me he loves me…and I just can't say it back. He's
getting mad at me."*

"I'm not sure what you want me to say, Laura." Actually, I think
I did know what she wanted. She was fishing for me to tell her that
I loved her. I'd stopped doing that a while back. Although I still
loved her in my own way and I was certain I probably would, I'm
not in love with her. If I tell her that I love her she will take it
differently than I mean it and I'd be just as guilty of dragging this
out as she was.

Trey was always telling me, "You just have to be honest
with her. Just tell her exactly how you feel. If she doesn't want to
accept that, it's not on you, man." Trey and I had this conversation
often. A lot of the times it was the same conversation we'd had the
week before. He's a good friend though, so every time I called he

SCOOTINAMERICA-INSIDE MY HELMET

picked up and he reinforced the things I already knew but needed to hear. He didn't sugarcoat things for me, he always shot straight from the hip and the result was slowly helping me untangle the mass of conflicting emotions inside of me. Once again I text Laura back and said,

What I finally told her was, *"Listen Laura, "I will always care about you. I want you to be happy and if this guy you're with does that for you that's great. I want to be your friend."*

"I don't want to be your friend. I can't be your friend. I need more than that."

"I can't give you more than that, Laura. I'm being as honest with you as I possibly can."

Having these conversations with her were emotionally wrenching and each one seemed to take a little more out of me. I knew Trey was right and the only way I would truly be free was to completely cut her off. She'd told me more than once that she doesn't want to be my friend. She's continued to prove to me that we don't really want the same things nor do we share the morals and values that I knew in my heart I wanted to live my life by. The only problem was making that big step...and at that point I just wasn't ready to do that...yet.

I pushed on through Oklahoma already disheartened because of my personal turmoil and the first few stops we made only amplified that feeling. The lack of participation was downright depressing and I'd begun to turn it inward and wonder if there was something that I could be doing better...or different. I was so used to succeeding. That drive was so ingrained in me that it was hard for me to learn to not take it personally when the bad days happened. From one stop to the next I had to spend a lot of time in my head drawing on past experience and when we showed up at a dealership where it seemed that the entire community had turned out, I once again had the proof I was seeking...people are good at heart. Not only were our hearts and donations buckets full, but

SCOOTINAMERICA-INSIDE MY HELMET

when the Warhorse broke down before we left Oklahoma, the dealership we were at graciously offered to fix it.

I'd been on the road for about five months by this time and I was learning something new every day. I was also evolving. What I was learning was changing me…for the better. The fact that something good happened every time I seemed to be at my lowest point was teaching me to be more optimistic and to not hang on to anxiety caused by things you can't change. You have to keep moving forward no matter what and never stop believing that you'll make it out the other side.

That sentiment was only strengthened when we got to Paris Texas and met a Vietnam Veteran named John. John wanted to ride with us for a couple of days and as we spoke I was looking at this vest he wore and I realized that pinned to it was not one…but two purple hearts.

"Can I ask you about the purple hearts?" He nodded and I said, "Do you mind telling me the story of how you got them?"

In a quiet, unassuming way he said, "It was a simple case of being in the wrong place…at the wrong time. I was nineteen years old and we were pushing in to take over Quảng Trị in Nam. On the way in I had a grenade thrown at me. It took me down. I woke up sometime later with an above the knee amputation on one side and a below the knee on the other." I had so many emotions running through me as he spoke that I wasn't sure which one to actually feel. Of course respect was at the top of the list.

"How old are you now, John?"

"I'm sixty-three. I'll be sixty-four next month."

"And you have worked your whole life and you still serve by riding with the Patriot Guard?"

"Yes sir."

111

SCOOTINAMERICA-INSIDE MY HELMET

"What kinds of things are the Patriot Guard involved in?"

"We volunteer to attend the memorial services of our active military, first responders and honorably discharged veterans among other things. We want to be there to ensure that they receive the dignity and respect they deserve."

"Wow, that's amazing. So do you have to be a veteran to be a part of the Patriot Guard?"

"No. It's a nationwide organization and the only thing we all have in common is a love of riding and a deep respect for those who have served."

Later that day John took us to the Red River Valley Veteran's memorial. As we walked through and read the names on the stone pavers and the benches he was stoic…but when he stood at the edge of the Ring of Honor and looked upon the names of those who were felled in battle I could see the reverence he held for these brothers and sisters of his in his eyes. It dawned on me that this is why he tells the story of coming home at nineteen without both of his legs as if he were talking about a simple trip to the emergency room. To a man like John this wasn't about him. He'd left a huge part of himself over there…but he'd come home. To John, this was about them…the fallen, the ones who never came home. Instead of asking for sympathy for what he's lost he appreciates what he still has…his life, and he's still living it. John didn't seem to fathom that he was one of the finest men this great country had produced. He didn't think of himself as a hero or someone to be honored. To him that right was reserved by those whose name this wall bore, and now his mission was about serving them. My mission on this trip is to make sure those children who are left behind because one or both of their parents answered the call of duty and made that ultimate sacrifice, have access to an education that can give them a step up in life. I knew that meant I was serving them too, and I knew that was going to give me a sense of pride and accomplishment…but what I felt most often since I began this trip was a sense of overwhelming gratitude. I'm so grateful to have this opportunity. I'm so grateful that I chose to

SCOOTINAMERICA-INSIDE MY HELMET

finally start living my life, and I'm so grateful that I'd chose to do it by honoring those who so richly deserved it.

****

When we arrived at Riders Harley Davidson in Trussville Alabama, it looked like they were getting ready for the party of the century and it turned out that they had set it all up for us. The place was decked out with a stage and live music, there was delicious food donated by one of the local restaurants and it looked like most of the community was there. I found out that they had been advertising for us before we got there and that they'd even set their own donation goal. They wanted to raise at least five thousand dollars for our cause between Riders HD and the city of Jasper Alabama. Melissa, the manager of Riders told me that the city of Jasper had put the word out over social media and they'd been asking for donations for weeks. That night after a great party where I met a lot of good people, Scooter and I were treated to a hotel room to sleep in…but that was only the beginning.

On day two of our trip into Alabama Scooter was treated to a "Spa Day" and me to a massage. After thousands of miles on the road we both needed and welcomed a little pampering. When it was time to leave the hotel and make the mile trip into downtown Jasper, twenty to thirty members of the local H.O.G. chapter met us and escorted us all the way down the interstate towards downtown. I was overwhelmed by all of the attention and good will that was being shown to us and I had nothing but good thoughts in my head. My escorts were using a lot of hand signals and because it's not something I'm really comfortable with, I chose to ride in the back and follow them. I was doing about sixty miles an hour on the interstate when the mounts that my GoPro sat on came loose and the whole thing flew off. I watched in shock in the rear view mirror as it hit the pavement and the pieces scattered in different directions. I was suddenly in a panic. I had to stop…I had to at least try and salvage what I could. That Go-Pro held five months of this journey…things I hadn't posted or talked about anywhere else. The footage I had on it was supposed to be for a documentary someday…not to mention it was my own personal diary. I'd poured my heart out to it after each phone call from Laura. The coyotes that I'd fought off were on there as well as the "bloody" motel room in Texas. I felt sick to my stomach and I signaled to one of the guys that I had to stop.

I pulled the bike over and walked back along the shoulder of the Interstate. At this point I was trying to tell myself that it would be okay. As long as I was able to salvage the SD card I'd still have all of the footage. I was trying not to think about the alternative...all of that irreplaceable footage lost. I started picking up the pieces of the camera that were scattered everywhere. As I found them I inspected each one closely and my anxiety increased each time I realized it wasn't the piece I was looking for. The SD card had popped out and it was gone. After several long, frantic minutes of searching I had to admit that to myself. I felt a deep sense of loss. I felt more agony over losing that little SD card then I felt over selling any of my things before leaving for this trip. The difference was that if I ever wanted more stuff I could buy it...but the footage I had on that card was gone forever. I knew I had to suck it up for now. I was being escorted into town like a VIP and people had put a lot of time and effort into this. I had to put a smile on my face for them, and get through this day.

When we got back on the road, our escorts led me off the interstate and into downtown Jasper where they had blocked off the main street to traffic. People lined the streets on either side and Firetrucks took over the lead with their ladders up. When we came to the end of the street in front of this little bar, Mayor Posey was there waiting to meet us. We parked our bikes and Scooter and I were asked to come up front. The Mayor gave a little speech about what the ride was all about and he also talked about what a great thing he thought it was. He said that Jasper is proud to be a part of it all...and then he presented me with a little glass case. Inside the case was the "key" to the city. I was choked up and once again amazed at how quickly things can change.

In just a few short minutes I'd gone from being heartbroken and feeling as if the weight of the world was on my shoulders back to knowing with absolute certainty that I was doing

SCOOTINAMERICA-INSIDE MY HELMET

the right thing here. Alexander Graham Bell said, *"When one door closes, another door opens; but we so often look so long and regretfully upon the closed door, that we do not see the ones which open for us."* I was learning not to dwell on that closed door, but to look towards the next open one instead. When I look back on this trip in years to come I will undoubtedly feel a twinge of regret that all of that footage was lost...but the memories will still be there and I get to hold onto those for a lifetime. I got a phone call not long after that which I would hold onto forever as well.

Still feeling a bit disheartened about losing the Go-Pro, I answered a call from my dad. As soon as I heard his voice I said,

"Dad what's wrong?" He sounded choked up...like he was holding back tears. My imagination was running wild. Was he sick? Is someone hurt?

"Nothing's wrong Adam...I just wanted to tell you something." Even though he was trying to put my mind at ease I had a feeling of foreboding.

"Okay...what is it, Dad? What's going on?"

"For five years now I've spent my days being taken out of bed every morning and put into my wheelchair. I'd sit there for hours and stare at the same spot on the wall before it was time to be put back to bed...just to start over again in the morning. It was a whole lot of nothing." He paused and I could tell he was gathering himself to go on. I waited and he did, "It's hard to describe...but I felt like I had lost sight of any value I had to anyone any longer. Then you decided to go on this trip and you asked me to be a part of it...and you saved me. Over the past several months I've actually begun to feel like the man I used to be again...and then some. I'm helping my son and I'm serving my country. I feel like a productive member of society and a very proud father. I just wanted to say thank you, Son. I'm so damned thankful."

115

SCOOTINAMERICA-INSIDE MY HELMET

I had to choke back my own tears as my father's words warmed and overwhelmed me. To this day hearing those words was hands down the proudest day of my trip…and maybe even my life. It's one thing to knowingly do a good deed, but to unwittingly have such a profound effect on the life of someone you love and respect is awe-inspiring. His words will forever live in a special place in my heart.

SCOOTIN AMERICA-INSIDE MY HELMET

A view of our ride into downtown Jasper Alabama

CHAPTER EIGHTEEN

"Life is either a daring adventure or nothing at all. Security is mostly a superstition. It does not exist in nature."—Helen Keller

In June of 2015 Harley Davidson museum opened their new exhibit, "Willie G. Davidson: Artist, Designer, Leader, Legend" in Milwaukee. In an effort to promote the exhibit Harley Davidson ran a "How Far Would You Ride?" campaign. The idea was to have riders gather in Green Bay and ride to Milwaukee for the opening. This campaign was right up my alley and since Green Bay is also my hometown, I thought it would be a great time to shoot a pilot episode for the documentary I've been thinking of doing. I signed up a film crew from Ohio to follow me for a week and they met me at the rally that day. I'd already done a couple of interviews for the local news stations and I was scheduled to meet the mayor. My buddy Blaster from Indiana was riding with me at that time. Blaster is a retired Senior Master Sergeant and the Indiana representative of the Combat Veterans Motorcycle Association, or the CVMA. In at least 90% of the states I've ridden through so far a representative of the CVMA has ridden along with me. They've been incredible and have helped us out with things like hotel rooms and meals and other things along the way.

The day the rally started in Green Bay things were chaotic. There were hundreds of people there and in the midst of all that was happening a young woman approached me. She told me her name was Julia and she went by "Harley Babe."

"We've messaged a few times," she reminded me.

"Oh yeah, you're from out West?"

"I'm from California, yeah. I'm just out riding the U.S. now like you and Scooter. I'm riding to promote women riders."

SCOOTINAMERICA-INSIDE MY HELMET

"That's great! You know, I'd love to talk to you and compare notes but there's a little too much going on today. Maybe we could meet up when things are less chaotic."

"Yeah sure."

The ride to Milwaukee was short and sweet and the city was literally full of bikers. I ran into Julia again as the guys and I were looking for a place to go out that night and invited her to come along. We found this cool little restaurant/bar downtown called, "The Safe house." It's a "spy" restaurant/bar and in order to even get in the door you have to know the password...or you have to do what they say. They can tell you to do all kinds of crazy stuff and the big catch is that you're part of the show. The people already inside the restaurant get to watch you on these big monitors as you make a complete, silly fool of yourself. I loved it!

We all made it inside and there were people wandering around on a scavenger hunt or looking for clues for one thing or the other. We were shown to a booth next to a bookcase. The wall behind us was covered with autographs of famous authors and I thought that was cool...and then the bookcase opened up, the booth spun around and suddenly we were sitting in the middle of the dance floor. It was awesome. We had a great time and I got to know a little more about Julia. At that point she'd been on the road for two months and when I saw what she was riding I cracked up. Julia is twenty-four years old, about five-foot-four and maybe a hundred and twenty pounds soaking wet. She's riding this huge Bagger and it's completely loaded down. It's hard to look at her and even imagine her being able to hold it up.

She rode with me for a couple of days and we talked a lot about what we were doing out here and how we were going about planning our trip. She told me she sort of felt like she was "drifting."

"I think I need more structure, like you," she said. "I can't get the dealerships to give me much attention at all."

SCOOTINAMERICA-INSIDE MY HELMET

"You know, the structure is good, for the most part, but it also has its drawbacks. My schedule has made this a job for me. I have to be certain places on certain days at certain times. It's a job…that I don't get paid for. So shoot for structure if that's what you need, but be careful not to lose sight of what you're doing."

I enjoyed our time together and we parted ways with plans to stay in touch and hopefully meet up again along the way. She took off to head for the East coast and Scooter and I were headed west to Minnesota.

****

I was at one of the dealerships in Minnesota when I met a lady named Diane. She was around fifty-five years old and riding a brand new 2015 HD Street Glide. She introduced herself and told me that she had a spare bedroom and Scooter and I were welcome to stay with her that night. I gratefully accepted. That night as we sat and talked I found out that Diane had been married for quite a few years. She came home one night to a note on her refrigerator from her husband. He'd left her a note to tell her he was leaving her. We bonded over the fact that we had both recently gone through a pretty devastating break-up. In my case I'd dealt with the pain by turning it all outward, partying and being social while feeling like I was breaking apart on the inside. Diane told me she did just the opposite. She turned her pain inward and she practically became a hermit. She only left the house for work and she'd stopped seeing a lot of her friends.

Diane and her husband were a Harley couple, but Diane didn't ride herself. She'd always ridden on the back of the bike. In an attempt at helping her get over the depression she was in after the break-up, some of her friends talked her into getting her motorcycle license. It was a great idea for a lot of reasons. Diane said it started by just giving her a sense of purpose…practicing and learning how to ride. Once she had her license it inducted her into a network of people across the nation. That's another one of the great thing about riding. The people are like one giant family and

SCOOTINAMERICA-INSIDE MY HELMET

it's a great way to make new friends and to find new, fun things to do.

When I left Diane I was still headed west. I was in this dealership up near the Minnesota/ North Dakota border when she suddenly appeared again. This time that new bike was loaded down with gear. "I want to go with you for a week," she said. "But, I want to do it like you…no hotels, no plans. I want to sleep where you sleep and eat what you eat."

I believed that she was serious, but skeptical that she'd make it an entire week. So far most of the men that wanted to ride with me have only made it for two or three days before they give up and head home to a warm bed.

"Are you sure?" I asked her.

"Yep, one week."

"Okay, you're in."

From there we headed on out into North Dakota. That evening we stopped at this little barbecue joint in the middle of nowhere. As we ate and the sun got close to going down behind the mountains she said,

"Um…where are we going to sleep?"

"I don't know. I haven't figured it out yet."

She laughed…nervously. "Oh…okay. When were you going to figure it out?"

"I tell you what; I'll do that right now." When the server came back I asked her, "Who owns this place?"

She told me the owner's name and then she said, "She's in the back cooking right now."

"Perfect. When she has a second can you ask her to come out and talk to me?" It wasn't long until the lady who owned the place came out from the back. I introduced myself, Diane and Scooter and then I told her my story. "Is there any chance we might be able to sleep out behind your restaurant tonight?"

"Sure, I have no problem with that."

I thanked her and then with a grin told Diane, "And there you go."

After we finished our meals we pulled the bikes around behind the little building. We were right at the edge of the woods and here was Diane with her brand new bike with the personalized plate that says, "Mr. Gray." I cracked up when I found out that's what she named her bike. I thought that was great.

She pitched her tent and I staked out my lean-to and I said, "Hey, since we're here for the night I think I'll see about getting us a few beers." I went back up to the restaurant and asked the owner where the nearest liquor store was at.

"It's a ways," she said. "Are you just planning on staying here for the night?"

"Yes."

"I can give you a six-pack," she said.

"Cool. Thank you."

Diane and I drank a couple of beers as we sat and talked. When it was time to turn in she went into her tent and I laid down in the lean to with Scooter. I was in bed for about two hours and the entire time I was getting feasted on by mosquitos. It was absolutely miserable. I finally couldn't take it any longer and I went over to her tent and knocked. She looked out at me and I said, "Can I come in?"

SCOOTINAMERICA-INSIDE MY HELMET

We sat up a while longer telling stories and she let us sleep in the tent that night. It was all perfectly innocent and I appreciated the hell out of it. The next day we continued on and I have to say I was wrong about Diane not making it. She not only made it the entire week, but she did it without complaint. Her bike, "Mr. Gray" was well-ridden by the end of that week. I'd taken her through the dirt and the mud and down more than a few back roads. We made it as far as Lake Superior together and I ended our week by stripping down to my shorts and jumping into the lake. It's all about the experience for me. Diane went home that day and I headed on towards Montana.

Harley Babe navigates her loaded down Street Glide

Diane riding by my side down the open road

CHAPTER NINETEEN

"The purpose of life is to live it, to taste experience to the utmost, to reach out eagerly and without fear for newer and richer experience." — Eleanor Roosevelt

Not long after Diane left and went home, I was in Missoula Montana when I got a call from Julia,

"Hey! I've got two weeks that I can ride with you. Where are you?"

"Great! I'm in Montana. Where are you?"

"Ohio. I was here visiting the camera crew."

"So how long will it take you to get here?"

"I'm not sure. I'll keep in touch along the way."

I was excited. Harley Babe coming back out to ride with me will be the first time since I started this trip that someone came back for a second round. I figured out how many miles away she was and calculated how long I thought it would be until she made it. I was thinking at least two days…boy was I wrong. From where Julia was to where she ultimately met up with me was 1360 miles. This crazy girl made it in one day. In all the years I've been riding I've never known anyone to drive that many miles in one day. I was impressed…and she was tired and hungry. I found a place for us to eat and had her food ordered by the time she got there.

We rode together from Montana on through Idaho and into Washington. It was really nice to have the company and like Diane, Harley Babe rode hard and didn't complain about a thing. She camped where I camped and ate what I ate and these two ladies were showing up just about any guy I'd ridden with so far.

SCOOTINAMERICA-INSIDE MY HELMET

We were out on this road one night and it was pitch black. I mean no moon, no stars…nothing. We were going really slowly because I kept worrying about deer. We'd already seen one alongside the road and I kept thinking one was going to dart out all of a sudden and I'd have no choice but to hit it. We finally came to this tiny little town and for some reason all of the hotels were packed. We stopped in at this little bar and I did like I always do, struck up a conversation and tried to find us a place to camp out. I asked the bartender if there was a campground around anywhere or if he knew of anywhere we could camp out for the night, but he wasn't the friendliest guy in the world and pretty much no help at all.

We finally left to just go out and look around. We found a park in the middle of town and we talked about camping there. I'm not sure why, but you know when you get that tingling sensation in the back of your neck and you just know that something's not right? That's how this place made me feel. I told Julia and we moved on, eventually coming up on a church. In my experience so far, churches have been good, safe places to stay. We parked the bikes but that's when I noticed a police cruiser moving down the street really slowly.

"Maybe we shouldn't unload the bikes just yet," I told Julia. "I really don't want to unpack and then have to pack it all back up because he tells us we can't stay here."

We waited, thinking he'd either come over and talk to us or he'd leave. He didn't do either, but he kept circling the block. Another cop joined him and then another. They all stopped near the intersection across the street and were standing there talking for about a half an hour. It was somewhere between two or three a.m., and I was exhausted and I finally said,

"The hell with this. I'm going to go over there and just ask them if it's okay if we camp here."

I walked across the street and I was a few feet away when one of the cops…a younger guy, startled. He pulled out his gun

SCOOTINAMERICA-INSIDE MY HELMET

and trained it on me and my hands went up. My heart was pounding in my chest. It's not a good feeling to look down the barrel of a service revolver. "What are you doing?"

"Hey man, I just wanted to ask you a question. We're just looking for a place to camp for the night." I gave him the abbreviated version of what I was doing and he lowered the gun.

"If you go down this road here and take a right there are a lot of little turn-outs where nobody will bother you."

"Perfect, thanks." I went back over and got Julia and we headed up the direction he'd told us to go. It was still pitch black...maybe even darker. We went slowly and looked for the turn-outs he was talking about, but we couldn't find any. The shoulder was really wide in places though so finally I pulled off onto it and told her, "We're just going to camp here." I was literally done for the night.

"Here? On the shoulder of the road?"

"I have to get some rest and you need some too."

"Okay." We set up our stuff and we camped right there. I made a video of it for my social media in the morning. I've slept in some strange places, but the shoulder of the road was a first for me.

****

Julia and I did Washington and when we were near the Washington/Oregon border and getting ready to head to Sturgis, I got a big surprise. Diane showed up at the dealership we were at. She was loaded down again and she said, "I'm going to ride with you for the next two weeks all the way to Sturgis." I looked at Julia and I could tell she'd known that Diane was coming.

"She messaged me and I told her where we would be," Julia said with a grin.

SCOOTINAMERICA-INSIDE MY HELMET

So here I was with two women who were saddled up and ready to do this and I had to put it out there on my Facebook page that these girls were showing up the boys in a big way. The path we were headed on took us through some rough terrain. We rode a lot of mountain trails and we rode hard. The ladies rode right along with me every step of the way and the most help they needed was the occasional push when we'd pick a spot to camp that was way off the beaten track. I can honestly say they have been the two hardest riders that have ridden with me this far, and once again, no complaints. We slept in a cow pasture one night for lack of a better place. We woke up the next morning, surrounded by the herd. The girls found that as funny and exhilarating as I did. We bathed in rivers in our underwear and we camped out behind convenience stores in town. I loved the hell out of the company and we were all learning things from each other.

At one point we'd met a nice couple who offered us a place to stay for the night. We graciously accepted and when we got to their place I told Julia… "You've got way too much stuff. We're going to lay it all out and I'm going to help you go through it and decide what you need to keep and what you have to get rid of, okay?"

"Okay." We laid it all out in the driveway of this couple's home. We went through it item by item.

"Do you really need this?" I'd ask her. Sometimes she'd just say no and other times she'd say,

"I really like that."

"When was the last time you used it?"

"Well…I haven't used it…yet."

I laughed. "You've been on the road now for three months. If you haven't used it, you don't need it."

SCOOTINAMERICA-INSIDE MY HELMET

Willingly, she gave up some items and reluctantly she gave up others…like a pair of jeans she really loved. We ultimately cleaned out about 20% of her stuff. "Now we need to box it up and mail it to wherever you want to mail it." Then I gave her a few items she needed but didn't have and when all was said and done her pack was so much lighter and easier for her to load on and off her bike.

From there we were headed into Wyoming. I knew ahead of time that there was a rodeo going on in Cody so I had my dad call ahead and see if he could get me on the books. It was another item I wanted to scratch off my bucket list. I wanted to ride a bull in the rodeo. He'd called back and told me the books were closed and he wasn't able to get me in. I wasn't going to let that discourage me though. My plan was to talk to them when I got there and see if there was any way I could still finagle it.

When we got into Cody the rodeo was already in full swing. I went to the admin booth and asked about getting on the books. They told me the same thing they'd told my father, the books were closed. They didn't seem willing to budge on it at all and I was disappointed. That night the girls and I went across the street from the rodeo grounds to a little tavern. There was this cowboy there and he was talking to everyone. He was telling these big, wild stories about rodeos he's been in and cowboys he's known. I introduced myself and the ladies and I told him what we were doing and about mine and Scooter's mission.

"That's awesome man. I know a lot of the people in the rodeo association here. I bet I can get you a big donation."

"That would be great, thanks. Are you riding in the rodeo?"

"Yes sir. I'm a professional saddle bronc rider."

"That's awesome. I really wanted to get on the books. I want to ride a bull…but the books were closed by the time we got here."

"I can get you in."

SCOOTINAMERICA-INSIDE MY HELMET

"Are you serious?"

He shrugged. "Sure, it won't be a problem at all. You'll have to wait until tomorrow to ride though. We'll build up what you're doing too and you'll get that donation as well, just watch."

I was ecstatic. "Wow, thanks! Get me in man; I'm ready to do this."

"Will do. Hey, I have me a big RV too. I brought a couple of girls with me and we're all staying in it, but ya'll are welcome to stay there for the night too if you need a place to stay."

I asked the ladies what they thought and we all agreed an RV was better than a campout on a chilly night in Wyoming. Since all we had to do is walk across the street, we stayed and enjoyed our drinks and listening to the cowboy's stories. The only thing that worried me was as the night went on and that cowboy got drunker…his stories got bigger and wilder. I didn't worry too much about it though, at least not right then. I was way too excited about tomorrow and finally getting to ride that bull.

**There is something liberating about bathing in a river
after riding the heat of the west**

CHAPTER TWENTY

"Only those who risk going too far can possibly find out how far they can go." — T.S Eliot

Since we didn't have to drive and we didn't have to go far that night, I'd imbibed in more alcohol than I usually would have. I was whiskey drunk and on top of that, we'd started drinking Fireball towards the end of the night as well. When it was time to leave the tavern, the four of us walked back over to the rodeo grounds. The cowboy took us out behind them to a make-shift little campground that was filled with a bunch of rusty old run-down campers. I didn't see an RV and I was beginning to re-think this whole thing again. Then...I spotted the "saddle bronc dummy." It was a barrel with an old towel riveted to it. You sat on this 55 gallon bucket and the towel was to give you the feeling of lifting (not pulling) on the rein while going through the motions. Getting on that thing may not have been one of my brighter ideas.

Get on it, I did though. I was having fun...right up until the time I got thrown. I sailed up about seven feet in the air and as gravity would have it...I came back down...right on a steel pipe. Searing fiery bursts of pain shot through me, beginning in my pelvis and pulsating through the rest of my body. Thank God for the alcohol because had I not been as buzzed as I was, I'd be willing to bet I would have felt it a lot more. I got up and shook it off. I was surrounded by people...cowboys who do this all the time...I wasn't going to lay down and cry.

After that, I was ready for bed. That's when the cowboy showed us to his "RV." As I followed him, each step I took amplified the pain in my hips and every freaking muscle in my body quivered. I was hoping at least a good night's sleep in a bed would help, but it looked like that wasn't going to happen either. This young cowboy might have looked at what he was offering us as a "recreational vehicle," but in actuality what it turned out to be was a busted up old camper that had been manufactured sometime in the 1970's.

The ladies and I gave each other looks like, "What the hell?" but, it was too late and we were all too tired to put any thought or conversation into it that night. I did notice there weren't any girl barrel racers around and I thought that was odd. Diane, Julia and I found a spot and went to sleep. If I thought I had been in pain the night before…it was a whole new world of it in the morning. I woke up savage blasts of it that I could feel all the way to my bones. I couldn't move to stand up. The girls helped me to my feet and got my boots on me that I couldn't bend over to put on. I went out to the hot, dusty dirty "campground" and I started walking it off.

As I was passing by the dodge pick-up truck that looked to be in almost as bad a shape as the camper I caught sight of one of the elusive barrel racers climbing out. "Hi." I told her who I was and about the cowboy offering us a place to stay. "Why aren't you in the Rig?"

She snorted. "This is it," she said. My fears about the cowboy were coming to light under the morning sun.

"Oh…well, where is the other girl?"

"What other girl?"

"He told us he was traveling with two girls, both barrel racers."

"Oh my God he is so full of shit. I am so sorry I agreed to come out here with him. After we get back I am so done."

He showed up about then and we all walked down to a little restaurant for breakfast. As soon as we got there the cowboy realized that he had "forgotten" his wallet. He just kept throwing kerosene on my suspicions. Something was definitely not right with this guy. I was torn because as much as I believed at that point that

SCOOTINAMERICA-INSIDE MY HELMET

he was full of shit...I still wanted to ride that bull. I was even
willing to do it with the crushing pain I was still feeling in my
pelvis. My hip was bruised now too and it had swollen up so big
that my jeans were tight and rubbing against it. I wanted to ride
that bull but I wondered if maybe it would turn out to be an even
less bright idea than the one I'd had about riding the dummy. I also
wondered if I should keep putting my trust in this guy who seemed
to tell one story after the other. Julia and Diane were sitting across
from me at the table so I text and said,

"There's supposed to be a storm coming in. Do you think
we should just take off now and head over to Sturgis?"

"That's probably a good idea."

"I just really want to ride that bull."

"Can you? I mean, you're obviously still in pain. You
grimace just when you stand up or sit down."

"Yeah...it hurts...but damn, I really want to do this."

We ate breakfast and the whole time the cowboy talked.
He was still talking about getting us a big donation, but I'd really
given up hopes of that happening. After breakfast I went off by
myself for a few minutes and called my dad. I told him about the
saddle bronc dummy and the pain I was having and then I said,
"But I really want to ride that bull and this guy says he can get me
on the books. I might not get a chance like this again."

"Adam if you're in that much pain what you need to do is
get to a doctor. What if something is broken?"

"It's bruised and swollen, Dad...but, I think if it was
broken I wouldn't be able to walk. I'm just not sure what to do."

"Listen to me, Adam. First off with that injury you do not
need to get on a bull. You're risking an even bigger injury and then
what? You'll have to cancel the rest of your trip maybe? Second of

SCOOTINAMERICA-INSIDE MY HELMET

all, that storm that's coming is slated to be a big one. The sooner you get on the road towards Sturgis, the safer your ride is going to be. Don't get on that bull, son."

As usual, my father was the voice of reason. I talked to the girls again and the consensus was that we needed to just saddle up our bikes and head out. I was probably more disappointed at that point than I would have been if I'd just accepted I couldn't get on the books in the first place…but hey, pretty much everything on this trip has started with a dream.

        ****

We started towards South Dakota underneath a blanket of dark clouds. As we rolled down the highways, the thunder rolled overhead. The sky seemed to keep coming down lower and it got to the point where it almost made me claustrophobic. The thunder changed from a roll to a loud, deep rumble as if it wanted to declare its raw power and maybe give fair warning of the wrath to come. A loud boom was what finally signaled the downpour we were suddenly caught up in. This was no ordinary rain storm. Chunks of hail rained down on us so hard that it could be heard thumping against the metal of the bike even above the roar of the engine. It was icy cold and it pierced everything it touched and sent a frigid chill throughout my body.

We pushed on and rode through it and by the time we made it to Sturgis the weather had cleared. I was surprised once more when we got there and Blaster showed up. The girls knew he was coming and they had all wanted to surprise me again. The four of us spent the next few nights partying and camping out underneath the stars. Blaster headed home after that and the girls and I headed out towards Indiana. Diane was with us for about another week before we had to part ways with her too. I'd gotten better with the good-byes since the day I had to say good-bye to G.I. Joe in New Orleans. It's mostly thanks to Julia and Diane. They've both come back twice now and they've helped me realize that it's not really a good-bye when it comes to a good friend. It's

SCOOTINAMERICA-INSIDE MY HELMET

only a "see you later," and I have the memories to hold onto as I look forward to when we meet again.

SCOOTINAMERICA-INSIDE MY HELMET

A perfect view of our trailer and the saddle bronc dummy

CHAPTER TWENTY-ONE

"Let's be cautious about relying so much on material things that we have no energy left for the spiritual aspects of our lives."--James A. Forbes

I was about three months from the end of my first year when many of my struggles began to come to a head. Foremost on my mind was the fact that we still had over two hundred dealerships on our list that we had yet to make it to. As I continued on with my journey the thought of where to go from here weighed heavily on my mind. When I stripped things down it looked like I had two options. I could continue the way I was going...doing personal appearances and getting to see the sights and meet the local people...or I could quite bluntly just hit the stops. I knew that if I rushed and concentrated only on making it from one dealer to the next that I could still finish hitting everyone on my list...but to what avail? Such a huge part of this mission had turned out to simply be about the people and this country. Although the kids we were helping by giving money to the American Legion didn't come second to any of that, I realized it was all a part of the same thing. Walking into a dealership and sitting a jar on the counter without giving anything of yourself was going to net a lot less donations than say going on a toy run or hanging out with the community as they come together and find new ways to encourage people to give. So, although completing our stops was still doable at that point, I didn't feel like it was the best option.

The second option...to keep going along as I was and hit as many as I could was also doable...but just as making the quick stops would, eliminating almost two hundred dealerships from our trip would be saying good-bye to tens of thousands...if not hundreds of thousands of dollars for the kids. I wasn't sure my conscience could live with that one either.

SCOOTINAMERICA-INSIDE MY HELMET

There was a third option…but it was one that I wasn't sure was even a viable one. We could go another year on the road. When I considered that one I knew that I was willing to dedicate another year…but there were two obstacles I'd have to overcome first. The first and most important was Scooter. By the end of that first year we would have completed most of the warmer states. Although we'd come across some extreme weather the first year, what we'd face the second one would make those look like sunny days. I knew without a doubt there was no way I could do that to Scooter. I'd had the idea of a chase vehicle on my mind from the start and there were some very kind and innovative people in the background of all of this that were willing to help me make that thought a reality. But, before any of that could happen I would have to figure out the other obstacle: funding. The chase vehicle would have to have a driver and gas and maintenance while on the road. None of that was likely to come cheap. Aside from that, I'd spent most of my own money this first year so another year on the road for me alone would be an issue if I didn't contract more sponsors.

I spent my days on the road and my nights lying awake and wrestling with all of that and I began once again reaching out to the generous people that have followed us and supported us all along. Ultimately none of it came easy but by November things had started to come together and the second year became a reality. The chase vehicle was on the road driven by a young lady who had served in the military and possessed the time, the motivation and the ability to continue to serve with us on the road. Scooter's comfort would be provided for and one of the heavy weights had been removed. The financing was still sketchy but every day we were gaining more followers and more donations and along with all of that came more people willing to sponsor us and help us out along the way.

With that settled I finally had the time to look within myself before I began the second year and revel in what I was taking away from the first. I'd learned so much about this gorgeous country…but along the way something happened that I hadn't even been banking on when I left. The journey that I thought was

SCOOTINAMERICA-INSIDE MY HELMET

about serving others had served me as well. It had become a journey of self-discovery and personal growth. I'd learned more about myself than I ever knew possible starting with finally finding that elusive key that would release the last of the binds which held me back from achieving absolute peace in my heart. I used that key to release myself from the hold that my relationship with Laura still had on me.

   I finally called the phone company and had her calls and texts blocked and then I blocked her from all of my social media sites. It was a huge step for me and it wasn't completely without pain. Cutting her out of my life had never been in the plan. I'd accepted long ago that we couldn't stay married but, I learned along the way that I had truly never really been happy. What I had with Laura was what I thought I wanted...what I thought was expected of me. But in reality what I'd had was a lover whose love language was completely different from mine. I was always willing to give Laura the love and attention she craved while we were together...and she was always willing to take it, while giving very little back in return. During my months on the road I'd met so many beautiful women and received so many messages telling me what a great guy they thought I was and how I'd make an amazing boyfriend or husband. My heart had been in so much pain following the divorce that although I heard what they were saying, I wasn't able to really process it and take it to heart. I could finally see that although all of these new doors were opening that I had yet to find it in myself to step through them. During one of the last conversations that I had with Laura it finally all fell into place.

   "Adam, don't you ever think about us getting back together?"

   I remember having to take a deep breath and tell myself that I was going to take one more stab at making her understand. "Laura, we will never be together in the way you're talking about again."

   She simply said, "You don't know that," as if it were a fact.

SCOOTINAMERICA-INSIDE MY HELMET

Still struggling for patience I said, "Yes Laura I do know that. The simple fact that you can take both marriage and divorce so lightly is a huge turn off to me. In your mind you think that all that we went through when we split up and divorced was not really a big deal because we can always get back together later on. It's almost like you're disconnected from reality." I think that aside from our personality differences that maybe our age difference was also coming into play here. However we got here, we had arrived and I finally accepted without a doubt that her reality and mine, her morals and mine and her values and mine were all different. I knew then that holding on to even a small part of it, would continue to hold me back from achieving the peace and happiness I'd been seeking.

This trip began with a dream and the need to give back. Coming into the end of the first year I realized that the old saying is right and it truly isn't about the destination, but the journey along the way. I'd not only found the fulfillment I sought by being allowed to serve others, I'd found the excitement that I'd been hoping for and an entire world that I hadn't even known existed had been opened up to me. I'd learned that the first step to moving forward was letting go, and that what we are told that we should want isn't always what we need.

As we grow up we're taught subtly by reading and watching television and most of all by seeing those around us that success is measured by what you possess. I'd learned that's a true statement. But possessions come in different forms. In the past the possessions I used to measure my success and my happiness were material ones. Striving for the nicest house and the newest car and that sixty-two inch screen television became tantamount to achieving that idea of success ingrained in my head. When I was at the point where I had all of that my soul continued to ache for more. I was forced to slowly come to the realization that instead of all of those things setting me free…they were doing the exact opposite. They were in fact holding my back by design. Letting go of all of that literally paved the road to my happiness.

SCOOTINAMERICA-INSIDE MY HELMET

While I was on the road I also learned that people are
genuinely good at heart. The things we see and hear in the media
sometimes make the world feel like a dark and hateful place. But
the reality is that those things are a miniscule part of what it's really
like. Most Americans genuinely love our country and their fellow
man. Most of them appreciate our freedoms and respect those who
fight for us. Most of them are willing to open up their hearts and
their homes to someone they believe is seeking to perpetuate those
freedoms in even the smallest sense. Most people, me included,
need to only "possess" a few things to make them truly happy. We
need to possess a sense of respect for ourselves and our fellow
man. We need to get to know our true selves and in doing that we
learn how to love and respect the people we are or to reshape the
people we want to become. I learned that the way to accomplish
this is to live life by that set of morals and values you hold onto
and to trust your heart and your conscience and you can never go
wrong.

I learned the difference in having material
happiness…which implies having money and things…none of
which will last forever, and having spiritual happiness. The former
only makes you want more. You want more things and more
money and the simple fact that it's never enough is the roadblock
to being truly happy. The latter, spiritual happiness implies
something else altogether. Spiritual happiness comes to those who
are both traditionally "rich" and "poor" alike. By the end of this
trip I was down to my last few dollars in the bank and everything I
owned could fit neatly on the back of my bike. But with that being
said, I'd never felt richer, happier or more at peace in my soul in
my life.

I was rich from the new friendships that I'd cultivated
along the way. I'd met people that had left their imprint on my soul
and literally changed my life forever. I had the hopes of seeing each
of them again someday…but if I didn't have that privilege, I knew
that I would always carry those valuable bits of them they'd shared
inside of me.

SCOOTINAMERICA-INSIDE MY HELMET

I was rich with strength. It had taken a great deal of it to overcome the pain I'd gone through when my marriage broke up. I'd had to find the strength to move on and the courage to give up a life that I'd always thought I'd wanted.

I was rich with all of the new knowledge I'd gained. I can't even list all of the things I learned; it was literally at least one new thing every day. But like the friendships and the strength, knowledge is something that I'd carry with me forever. It can't be bought or sold. It's mine to possess and cultivate.

Most of all at the end of this first year I was aware of something that I hadn't really believed about myself in the past. I'm rich in character. My values and my morals are what drive me now and when I wake up in the morning be that along the shoulder of the road, in a motel room or in the home of a kind-hearted person, I wake up feeling good about myself and with no qualms about looking at myself in the mirror. That doesn't mean I don't believe I still have work to do. We're all a work in progress and I look forward to more growth and discovery on our next year on the road as well as the years to come after that. Most important of all I look forward to the day when I can spend the holidays with my own family, surrounded with the riches of love and warmth and I can tell the stories of mine and Scooter's adventures on the road to the people who finally come into my life and complete me once and for all.

SCOOTINAMERICA-INSIDE MY HELMET

55727968R00082

Made in the USA
Middletown, DE
12 December 2017